Best wishes as you work toward
your eternal future!

With Love,
Karen & Bonnie
Feb. 10, 99

Lord I WOULD FOLLOW THEE

BRENT L. TOP

Bookcraft
Salt Lake City, Utah

"Lord, I Would Follow Thee," lyrics by Susan Evans McCloud, music by K. Newell Dayley. © The Church of Jesus Christ of Latter-day Saints. Used by permission.

Library of Congress Catalog Card Number: 96-85274
ISBN 1-57008-265-0

Second Printing, 1997

Printed in the United States of America

Savior, may I learn to love thee,
Walk the path that thou hast shown,
Pause to help and lift another,
Finding strength beyond my own.
Savior, may I learn to love thee—
Lord, I would follow thee.

Who am I to judge another
When I walk imperfectly?
In the quiet heart is hidden
Sorrow that the eye can't see.
Who am I to judge another?
Lord, I would follow thee.

I would be my brother's keeper;
I would learn the healer's art.
To the wounded and the weary
I would show a gentle heart.
I would be my brother's keeper—
Lord, I would follow thee.

Savior, may I love my brother
As I know thou lovest me,
Find in thee my strength, my beacon,
For thy servant I would be.
Savior, may I love my brother—
Lord, I would follow thee.

(Susan Evans McCloud, in *Hymns,* no. 220.)

CONTENTS

PREFACE

This book is a personal sojourn. It reflects my own innermost struggle to better understand what it means to become more like the Master, and if and how such emulation can be obtained. This project has been much different from any other book or article that I have written previously. In the past I have pondered and studied a subject and then have taught in my classes at Brigham Young University the concepts I have learned. Usually it is at that point that someone will say to me, "Brother Top, you really ought to write that up so that others can benefit from what you are teaching us." Writing refines my ideas, and the end product usually ends up better than what I had originally started with in my classroom. Virtually everything I have written before came upon the suggestion, prodding, and encouragement of others, with the intent that what I would say might actually help readers. This project has been different, however. This has been for me. If others benefit from what this book has to say, then that is just icing on the cake, but I needed to do this book—for me.

For many years I have read and pondered the following Book of Mormon passage: "Therefore, what manner of men [and women] ought ye to be? Verily I say unto you, even as I am." (3 Nephi 27:27.) I have often wondered if it was even possible to *be* like

Christ, even though I understood that through his atonement I could *become* like him in the resurrected, glorified, exalted sense. What caused me to think even more deeply about this process of being more like Jesus was the counsel of President Howard W. Hunter:

> One of the most important questions ever asked to mortal men was asked by the Son of God himself, the Savior of the world. To a group of disciples in the New World, a group anxious to be taught by him and even more anxious because he would soon be leaving them, he asked, "What manner of men ought ye to be?" Then in the same breath he gave this answer: "Even as I am." (3 Nephi 27:27.)
>
> The world is full of people who are willing to tell us, "Do as I say." Surely we have no lack of advice givers on about every subject. But we have so few who are prepared to say, "Do as I do." And, of course, only One in human history could rightfully and properly make that declaration. History provides many examples of good men and women, but even the best of mortals are flawed in some way or another. None could serve as a perfect model nor as an infallible pattern to follow, however well-intentioned they might be.
>
> Only Christ can be our ideal, our "bright and morning star" (Revelation 22:16). Only he can say without *any* reservation, "Follow me; learn of me; do the things ye have seen me do. . . ."
>
> The great standard! The only sure way! The light and the life of the world! How grateful we should be that God sent his Only Begotten Son to earth to do at least two things that no other person could have done. The first task Christ did as a perfect, sinless Son was to redeem all mankind from the Fall, providing an atonement for Adam's sin and for our own sins if we will accept and follow him. The second great thing he did was to set a perfect example of right living, of kindness and mercy and compassion, in order that all of the rest of mankind might know how to live, know how to improve, and know how to become more godlike.
>
> Let us follow the Son of God in all ways and in all walks of life. Let us make him our exemplar and our guide. We should at every opportunity ask ourselves, "What would Jesus do?" and then be more courageous to act upon the answer. We must follow Christ, in the best sense of that word. We must be about his work as he was about his Father's. We should try to be like him, even as the Primary children sing, "Try, try, try" ("Jesus Once Was a Little Child," *Children's Songbook,* p. 55). To the extent that our mortal powers

> permit, we should make every effort to become like Christ—the one perfect and sinless example this world has ever seen. . . .
>
> We must know Christ better than we know him; we must remember him more often than we remember him; we must serve him more valiantly than we serve him. Then we will drink water springing up unto eternal life and will eat the bread of life.
>
> What manner of men and women ought we to be? Even as he is. (In Conference Report, April 1994, pp. 83–84.)

President Hunter's words, as well as his humble spirit and Christlike example, touched me deeply. It was as if he had issued that charge personally and specifically to me. His challenge to "make every effort to become like Christ" still echoes in my ears. I knew I could do and be better, even though I felt that most of the "big sins" that would prevent Christlike discipleship had been eliminated from my life. Now I wanted to know what "small things"—practical, day-to-day-living kinds of things—I needed to do to remember the Lord more, know him better, and serve him more valiantly. That was the catalyst for change, but the change itself has come more slowly and has been a somewhat painful, difficult, self-disclosing process.

My own children have also made this personal sojourn to deeper discipleship difficult by their pointed and poignant reminders of my many weaknesses. If I became impatient or grouchy or less kind than I should be, one of them would say, "And you're writing a book about becoming more like Christ?" They reminded me quite often that my own life falls far short of his perfect example. My response, however, was, "Be patient with me. I am trying." That is why I needed to write this book. I need to keep trying—though I fall short more often than not. I need to focus my own mind, soul, and actions more on the "little things" that I need to do to be more like Christ. Elder Neal A. Maxwell said, "Moroni declared the need for us to deny ourselves 'all ungodliness' (Moroni 10:32), thus including both large and small sins. While boulders surely block our way, loose gravel slows discipleship too. Even a small stone can become a stumbling block." (In Conference Report, April 1995, p. 88.) This reminds me that even if my sins are like loose gravel and not big boulders, I still need to keep "trying to be like Jesus."

I'm trying to be like Jesus;
I'm following in his ways.
I'm trying to love as he did,
In all that I do and say.

At times I am tempted to make a wrong choice,
But I try to listen as the still small voice whispers,

"Love one another as Jesus loves you.
Try to show kindness in all that you do.
Be gentle and loving in deed and in thought,
For these are the things Jesus taught."

I'm trying to love my neighbor;
I'm learning to serve my friends.
I watch for the day of gladness
When Jesus will come again.

I try to remember the lessons he taught.
Then the Holy Spirit enters into my thoughts, saying,

"Love one another as Jesus loves you.
Try to show kindness in all that you do.
Be gentle and loving in deed and in thought,
For these are the things Jesus taught."

(In *Children's Songbook*, pp. 78–79.)*

In response to President Hunter's charge to emulate the Savior in all aspects of life, this book deals with three specific areas: personal life, relationships with others, and leadership. The questions that I asked of myself—How can I be a more Christlike person? How can I love others as he loves me? How can I be more like the Good Shepherd as I minister to others in my service and

---

leadership callings in his kingdom?—guided this project, and the book reflects what I discovered from studying the scriptures, researching what latter-day prophets have taught, and listening to the promptings of the Spirit (see D&C 52:9). I am not sure that I have anything to say that will benefit others or contribute to the body of knowledge already extant, but I have learned many things that I can and should be doing in my own life. This project has taught me that despite what progress I have made in my life, I am still quite a lot like the commandment-keeping, rich young ruler who asked Jesus, "What must I do to inherit eternal life?" The Savior reminded this young man, as well as me, that there were still many things lacking (see Matthew 19:16–22). It is in these areas of what I yet lack where I must think more often of the Savior—of what he would do and what he would have me do.

This has been a most difficult project. One of the things that has made it so difficult for me is the fear that others may consider me presumptuous to write such a book. And I fear that those who know me may say, like my children have, "How can *you* write a book on this subject?" I fear that some may perceive this as Brent Top saying, "Do as I say, not as I do." I have been heavily weighed down with these fears, but something overpowers even these daunting apprehensions—the knowledge that I needed to write this book for me. Learning to be more Christlike in even small ways is as important for me as it is for my family, my ward members, or my students. This has been a difficult inventory-taking job. I have had to see what I have in my life, what I need to acquire, and what I need to get rid of. "Meek introspection may yield some bold insights!" observed Elder Maxwell. "For example, we can tell much by what we have already willingly discarded along the pathway of discipleship. It is the only pathway where littering is permissible, even encouraged. In the early stages, the debris left behind includes the grosser sins of commission. Later debris differs; things begin to be discarded which have caused the misuse or underuse of our time and talent." (In Conference Report, October 1995, p. 29.)

Despite my feelings of total unworthiness and inadequacy to write a book like this on such a vital and noble topic, I have been blessed, as well as chastened and sobered, by this project. It has increased my love for the Savior and my desire to become more like him. I am sure that I will fall far short in my feeble attempts, but at least I'm trying. And as I try, my commitment to discipleship has been strengthened; and I have come to know that if we will at least try, the Lord will help us in our own personal quest to become more like him. As I feel more love for the Savior and more love from him, my innermost desire is to follow him, become more like him, and serve and love others with charity, the pure love of Christ. Like Peter and Andrew, who immediately left their fishing nets and followed the Master, I too desire with all my heart to respond affirmatively to his invitation to "come, follow me." I want to follow him to learn of him, to be healed by him, to be loved by him; but most of all I desire to become like him.

"Come, follow me," the Savior said.
Then let us in his footsteps tread,
For thus alone can we be one
With God's own loved, begotten Son.

"Come, follow me," a simple phrase,
Yet truth's sublime, effulgent rays
Are in these simple words combined
To urge, inspire the human mind.

Is it enough alone to know
That we must follow him below,
While trav'ling thru this vale of tears?
No, this extends to holier spheres.

Not only shall we emulate
His course while in this earthly state,
But when we're freed from present cares,
If with our Lord we would be heirs.

We must the onward path pursue
As wider fields expand to view,
And follow him unceasingly,
Whate'er our lot or sphere may be.

For thrones, dominions, kingdoms, pow'rs,
And glory great and bliss are ours,
If we, throughout eternity,
Obey his words, "Come, follow me."

(John Nicholson, "Come, Follow Me,"
in *Hymns,* no. 116.)

I wish to express my love for my wife, Wendy, and my appreciation for her patience with me and for her example to me. In this personal sojourn toward greater spirituality and more devoted discipleship, she has motivated me by her example, teachings, and love. I thank my children for their frequent reminders of my weaknesses, even though it hasn't always been comfortable to be taught from "out of the mouth of babes." If only one benefit could come from this challenging project of personally applying President Hunter's charge to follow the Savior in all aspects of life, I hope it would be that I become a better husband, father, and friend, and a more humble servant of the Lord in his kingdom.

Brent L. Top

1

Ye are a light of the world. A city that is set on an hill cannot be hid. Neither do men light a candle and put it under a bushel, but on a candlestick; and it giveth light unto all that are in the house. Let your light so shine before men, that they may see your good works, and glorify your Father which is in heaven.
—Matthew 5:14–16

Being an Example

Reflecting the Light of Christ Within Us

Several years ago my wife and I were sitting in the gate area of the Salt Lake City airport, awaiting the boarding call for our flight to a distant city on a speaking assignment for Brigham Young University. The flight had been briefly delayed, and so, to treat my perpetual case of impatience, I walked the length of the corridor to the Mrs. Field's Cookies shop to buy a treat. I had only enough change in my pocket for one cookie. At first I was sorely tempted to just gobble down the cookie, but I had already told my wife where I was going, and it would have looked pretty selfish to return empty-handed. So, struggling to overcome the "natural man," I returned to where Wendy was sitting and broke the cookie in half, and she ate one part and I ate the other. I really didn't think much of it (other than I wished I had had a few more cookies), until a woman approached us as we were getting ready to board the plane. "I thought you would be interested in knowing that my daughter has been watching you closely," she told us. "She said to me, 'That man must love that woman a lot.' When I asked her why she thought that, she responded, 'Because he had a cookie and broke it in half and gave her the big piece.' "

I was quite taken aback that someone had been watching us so closely, but I was grateful that I hadn't done anything stupid or sinful that would have reflected poorly on me, my wife, BYU, or the Church. On the flight I could not get this little episode out of my mind. My first reaction was one of relief: *Whew, I lucked out on that one.* Then I found myself mentally patting myself on the back: *Good job, Top. You are quite the gentleman—and a loving husband to boot.* That thought quickly dissipated when I realized that I could have just as easily, without even thinking, given Wendy the smaller piece of cookie.

My mind was flooded with scriptures and applications of what this seemingly insignificant event really meant. Two important lessons were driven forcefully home to my heart as I pondered the real meaning of the message that had come from "out of the mouth of babes."

1. We are never "all alone," and no act goes unseen. Just as I had no inkling that anyone would pay any particular attention to the simple act of sharing a cookie with my wife, so we often think that "no one will ever know" if we do something in private or without any particular fanfare. If a mugger had pulled a gun on Wendy and me while we waited for our flight and had demanded my wallet, I would have expected people to notice—but sharing a cookie? No. Similarly, we are more circumspect in what we say or do when we fully expect people to take note of who we are and what we are doing. But when we think we are all alone or that no one is paying attention or really cares, we may let our guard down, and then be surprised that we were not alone after all, but were seen and taken note of.

I thought how the young girl in this episode in a small way symbolized the way our Heavenly Father watches us. We may think we are all alone or that no one would ever know, but even our smallest, seemingly insignificant acts are seen. "I say unto you that mine eyes are upon you," declared to the Lord. "I am in your midst and ye cannot see me." (D&C 38:7.) Just as it was sobering for me to realize that this child had been watching me closely, I am sobered, but also motivated to be better, when I hear the

Lord's voice resounding in my mind and heart: "Hearken, . . . saith the voice of him who dwells on high, and whose eyes are upon all men" (D&C 1:1).

2. *Even seemingly unimportant acts may be significant.* Sharing a cookie may have seemed insignificant or a "little thing" to me, but to an observant and sensitive child that "little thing" was a "big thing" because it represented the deep love a husband had for his wife. Similarly, everything we do in life, whether it be good or bad, simple or profound, has an effect or influence on someone—either ourselves or others. "Be not weary in well-doing, for ye are laying the foundation of a great work," the Lord told the early Saints. "For out of small things proceedeth that which is great." (D&C 64:33.) The meaning of this passage for me is not just that the Church, which began small, would indeed one day become great; but, more important, that small things—actions, words, deeds that we may think are "no big deal"—may, in fact, powerfully affect another, either positively or negatively. And even if we don't think that our actions may influence another, we are reminded that there are no small things to the Lord in his assessment of who and what we really are, for our entire life and spiritual character is made up of a lifetime of small things. For this reason the Lord has declared that in his judgment of mankind, "whatsoever a man soweth, that shall he also reap" (Galatians 6:7). Nothing is "tossed out" in the Lord's spiritual weighing of our lives—everything is significant. Teaching his son Corianton concerning the justice and mercy of God, Alma said:

> And it is requisite with the justice of God that men should be judged according to their works; and if their works were good in this life, and the desires of their hearts were good, that they should also, at the last day, be restored unto that which is good.
>
> And if their works are evil they shall be restored unto them for evil. . . .
>
> Therefore, my son, see that you are merciful unto your brethren; deal justly, judge righteously, and do good continually; and if ye do all these things then shall ye receive your reward; yea, ye shall have mercy restored unto you again; ye shall have justice restored unto you again; ye shall have a righteous judgment restored unto you again; and ye shall have good rewarded unto you again.

> For that which ye do send out shall return unto you again, and be restored. (Alma 41:3–4, 14–15.)

In the Sermon on the Mount, Jesus compared his disciples to "a city set on an hill" that is noticeable to all around, even from many miles away. Like that city, Christ's disciples must let their light—their lives, their every word and action, their very being—"so shine before men, that they may see your good works, and glorify your Father which is in heaven." (Matthew 5:14, 16.) Through the years I have read that scripture and taught it in many different settings. Usually, however, I have said to my own children or to students something to this effect: "Be a good example so that you can be a positive influence on people and they will think well of you and the Church." I must admit that there have been times when I would casually say, "Let your light shine," in a way that may connote something more akin to "Be on your best behavior" or "Don't forget your manners" or "Don't burp in public." After the episode with the mother and daughter in the airport, I have come to realize that since we are really never all alone—since every action we do is seen and noted, and even seemingly trivial actions may be significant—Jesus' admonition to let our light so shine is more encompassing than I ever imagined.

Letting my light shine before men is not like turning on a light when I go into a room and turning it off when I leave. Neither is it like putting on a white shirt and tie when I sit on the stand in my priesthood leader "uniform" and then taking it off again when I am not "on display." I have come to realize that "a city set on an hill" is seen all the time, whether it wants to be or not; it can't just drop down into the valley whenever it so desires. A disciple of Christ reflects that light as much when he is cut off in rush-hour traffic, when he is in his grubbies working in the yard, or even when he is tired and irritable at home after a hard day at work, as when he is sitting on the stand in Church or sharing the gospel with his nonmember friends.

The light we hold up for all the world to see is our entire life—inward and outward, small and great, good and bad—not just the parts we want to highlight or our "greatest hits," the episodes when we were on our best behavior. Whether we like it or not, the light that we hold up is the "whole load of hay." It is every aspect of our life. Letting our light so shine, or being a true example, cannot be faked. "Be thou an example of the believers," Paul counseled Timothy, "in word, in conversation, in charity, in spirit, in faith, in purity" (1 Timothy 4:12). The Apostle Paul's usage of the word *conversation* in the context of being an example of the believers is most significant. The Greek word from which *conversation* is translated is *anastrophe*, which refers to one's whole manner of life. Letting our light shine before men cannot be compartmentalized; it requires a godly walk in all aspects of our lives. Only then can our examples influence others to "glorify [our] Father which is in heaven" (Matthew 5:16).

Sometimes when I have taught teenagers and young adults about the importance of being a good example so that others may think well of us and be influenced by our actions, someone would ask, "Why should we care what others think of us?" These young people seemed to equate the scriptural injunction "let your light so shine" with a conscientious attempt to impress people. Many seemed to think that seeking to impress people by our example was shallow at best and hypocritical at worst. As I pondered their comments and tried to formulate a response, I came to realize that Jesus was not asking us to put on a show to impress others by our actions. Neither was he charging us to be overly concerned about what others think of *us*. The light we are to let shine before men is not intended to draw the gaze and attention of others to ourselves, but rather to Christ. "It is not that I care what others think of me," I explained to my students, "as much as I care deeply about what others may think of the Savior and Heavenly Father *because* of me."

The resurrected Christ declared, "Behold I am the light which ye shall hold up—that which ye have seen me do" (3 Nephi 18:24). It is this Light that our lives must reflect in order to lead others to "glorify [their] Father which is in heaven." Being an example is not trying to impress others or even trying to influence or lead others. It is done whether others see us or not. Letting "the Light" be reflected in us is the natural by-product of taking Christ's name upon us and having his image graven upon our countenances. The degree to which our example lights the way for others is proportionate to the degree to which the "Light of the World" radiates in us. I don't have to consciously seek to be an example. If I love the Lord Jesus Christ with all my heart and seek to follow him, his light, life, and love will be reflected in me. In this manner we can let our light shine to the world whether we are alone or seen by millions. Recognizing that the Light we are to reflect is in very deed the Savior, we will understand the profound effects that our positive and negative personal examples have on how others will receive the power of Christ's teachings and love into their own lives.

The Damaging Effects of a Bad Example

Several years ago I had a long heart-to-heart discussion with my brother who had left the Church many years earlier. I was seeking to better understand what had led to his alienation from the Church in which he had been raised so that perhaps I could help him in some way. It was an ideal teaching situation, but it was my brother who taught me, not the other way around. He spoke at great length of hurt feelings he had incurred in his youth and of the bad behavior and hypocrisy he had seen in the lives of people who were viewed as "good Mormons" or who held positions of leadership or prominence in our LDS community. I had heard his stories many times before and felt that he was merely scapegoating others to cover his own misconduct that led to his estrangement from the Church.

"Well, you can't judge the Church by its people," I somewhat smugly responded, having heard this argument stated by others. I was trying to get the bad examples of others off the hook and make him responsible for his feelings and behavior.

"You *must* judge the Church by its people," he emphatically responded. "What good is the Church if it doesn't affect the lives of its members?"

This deeply affected me, and I have thought of it many times in the years since. My brother helped me to better realize that it really is impossible to separate a person's actions and attitudes from the gospel teachings he espouses. It is not just me that people will judge by my bad example and hypocrisy, it will also be that which I claim to be the major influence in my life—that which I claim to be my guiding light—the gospel. And in the end, since it is the Lord's name I have taken upon myself, my actions cannot help but affect how others may view him. While I don't believe my brother's inactivity can be totally blamed on the bad examples of others, I am deeply saddened that some may have never even known that a young man in their ward or neighborhood noticed them and recognized that their lives didn't measure up to their professed beliefs. If the Lord wasn't that important to them, as evidenced by their whole manner of life, how did they expect the Lord to be important to those whom they taught and led?

As Alma went forth proclaiming the gospel to those who were not in the Church, he learned that no matter how diligently he labored or how eloquently he preached, the success of his missionary endeavors was linked to how well the members of the Church reflected the light of Christ's gospel in their own lives:

> And it came to pass in the eighth year of the reign of the judges, that the people of the church began to wax proud, because of their exceeding riches, and their fine silks, and their fine-twined linen, and because of their many flocks and herds, and their gold and their silver, and all manner of precious things, which they had obtained by their industry; and in all these things were they lifted up in the pride of their eyes, for they began to wear very costly apparel.
>
> Now this was the cause of much affliction to Alma, yea, and to many of the people whom Alma had consecrated to be teachers, and priests, and elders over the church; yea, many of them were sorely grieved for the wickedness which they saw had begun to be among their people.
>
> For they saw and beheld with great sorrow that the people of the church began to be lifted up in the pride of their eyes, and to set their hearts upon riches and upon the vain things of the world, that they began to be scornful, one towards another, and they began to persecute those that did not believe according to their own will and pleasure.
>
> . . . There began to be great contentions among the people of the church; yea, there were envyings, and strife, and malice, and persecutions, and pride, even to exceed the pride of those who did not belong to the church of God.

> . . . And the wickedness of the church was a great stumbling-block to those who did not belong to the church; and thus the church began to fail in its progress.
>
> . . . Alma saw the wickedness of the church, and he saw also that the example of the church began to lead those who were unbelievers on from one piece of iniquity to another. (Alma 4:6–11.)

Perhaps every full-time missionary can testify of how some nonmembers will use the bad example of a "Jack Mormon" (or worse yet, one who professes total commitment to the Church) as justification for their unwillingness to hear the gospel message. We can see examples all around us that personify the maxim "I cannot hear what you are saying, because what you are doing is ringing louder in my ears." Truly, "actions speak louder than words," and bad actions on the part of those who profess to be disciples of Christ do much to cause others to dismiss the good words that they may hear. "For when they saw your conduct," declared Alma to his wayward son Corianton, "they would not believe in my words" (Alma 39:11). I believe that when we take upon us the name of Christ and covenant to always remember him, we agree to let our lights so shine by living our lives in such a way as to reflect him and the way his teachings, love, and atoning sacrifice have transformed us. In this manner we then can "stand as witnesses of God at all times and in all things, and in all places" (Mosiah 18:9). I believe that by virtue of that covenant, we will be held accountable not only for how our personal example affects those who do not have the gospel, but also for those members of the Church who may be influenced by such an example. There are many in the Church who are weaker in the faith, who may lack a strong gospel foundation at home and are easily influenced by others. They may look to those whom they perceive to be good Latter-day Saints and then justify their actions based on the examples they see.

I saw this principle in real-life application after our family moved to Utah from the East Coast. While we lived in the East, my children were the only members of the Church in their school. Their friends knew of their values and high standards and would many times try to improve their own behavior and vocabulary while being around my children. At other times they might say something to the effect of "You don't want to listen to this joke" or "You can't come with us to this movie because we know that you wouldn't approve." There were clear lines of demarcation between good and evil. My children knew which kids they should play with and which they should stay away from.

When we came to Utah, the lines became blurred. My children often expressed dismay that the kids who went to Primary or Young Women with them were the same young people who used the most foul language, broke the Word of Wisdom, or participated in other unworthy behaviors. It was disturbing to them that some of the kids from the "best homes," those who served in leadership positions at Church or seminary, or those who bore testimony on Fast Sunday and blessed the sacrament each week were some of the very kids whose behavior during the week bore no resemblance to gospel standards. After the shock of this wore off, my children then succumbed to rationalizing: "Why can't I go to that movie? The bishop's daughter is going to be there," or, "Why can't I date before I'm sixteen? All the girls in my class are dating." I believe that because the Lord has given us the charge to hold up our light unto the world, we will be held accountable not only for our sins but also for how we knowingly lead others into the pathway of sin or unknowingly influence others to rationalize their behavior because of our bad examples. I think the Apostle Paul was referring to this very principle when he taught the Roman Saints to guard their words and actions and "not to do anything that would make your brother stumble, or fall into sin" (Romans 14:13, *Today's English Version;* see also 1 Corinthians 8:9–13).

Avoiding Being a Bad Example Is Not the Same as Being a Good Example

"Behold, do men light a candle and put it under a bushel?" the Savior asked his disciples. Answering the question for them, he then declared, "Nay, but on a candlestick, and it giveth light to all that are in the house." (3 Nephi 12:15.) Putting a bushel basket over a candle would probably extinguish the flame. Similarly, continually living a life that does not truly reflect the Savior and his teachings stifles spiritual growth in ourselves and others. A bad example is like a bushel over a candle. Jesus was not just admonishing his followers to stay away from bushel baskets, but to hold up their light for all to see.

I remember as a child in Primary singing the familiar song: "This little light of mine, I'm going to let it shine, let it shine, let it shine." The chorus of this simple children's song reminds us that we must let our light—however little, however simple—truly shine forth, illuminating the way for others. Likewise, I think Jesus is saying to us that it is not enough to avoid being a "non-example"; rather, to truly follow him we can be neither wicked nor neutral—we must reflect the Savior in our lives so that others will never misunderstand what we believe, what we are committed to, and who it is we seek to follow. I learned this lesson in a most profound yet somewhat painful and embarrassing way.

During my senior year in high school I became acquainted with a young man who was not a member of the Church. We played on the varsity basketball team together. He was an underclassman, and so I would often tease him in practice and remind him that his job on the team was to "pass the ball to me and rebound when I shoot." We went on trips together with the team and experienced all the ups and downs of the season together. I thought we knew each other pretty well. After I graduated and went away to college, I learned from a friend that this same young man had become interested in the Church. He began attending seminary and Church activities and later took the missionary lessons, which culminated in his baptism. I later learned that he had been called on a mission. I was thrilled by his spiritual progress.

Several years later, after I was married, I ran into him again—the first time since our high school basketball-playing days. He had served a faithful mission and had since been married in the temple and was doing great. I was excited to see him and told him how happy I was with his joining the Church and the success he had experienced in life. I made some comment such as, "I just wish I had been the one to introduce you to the Church and to teach you the gospel." His response cut to the very core: "Brent, to tell you the truth, I didn't even know you were a member of the Church."

His words hit me hard. I had not been a bad example to him. I didn't break the Word of Wisdom or live the wild life of drugs, drinking, and immorality that so many LDS kids did. I had good friends and was active in the Church. I was even an Eagle Scout and had danced in the regional dance festival. How could he say that he didn't even know that I was a member of the Church?

I came to realize that it wasn't a bad example that caused my friend to think that, but rather it was that I had not been letting my light really shine. I was avoiding bad behavior, but my life did not clearly and unquestionably reflect what I stood for and what was important to me. I had not put a bushel over the light, but neither had I placed that light on a candlestick so that others could see the Light through me. I was a nonexample. I guess I was guilty of the very thing the Lord condemned when he declared: "I know thy works, that thou art neither cold nor hot: I would thou wert cold or hot. So then because thou art lukewarm, and neither cold nor hot, I will spue thee out of my mouth." (Revelation 3:15–16.) I didn't want to be a bad example that would influence others to do evil, but neither did I want to be "too good" or be viewed as a goody-goody. In the end, my life, what I really was, reflected no light bright enough to lead others to "glorify [their] Father which is in heaven."

I don't think my example is unique. I see many people in the Church, particularly young people, who seek to straddle the line between putting their light under a bushel and holding it high on a candlestick for all to see. This common character trait—appearing to be less than we really are—is a form of hypocrisy that prevents us from standing as witnesses of Christ "at all times and in all things, and in all places" (Mosiah 18:9). President N. Eldon Tanner said:

> Harry Emerson Fosdick observed that there are two kinds of hypocrisy: when we try to appear better than we are, and when we let ourselves appear worse than we are. We have been speaking of the

> kind of hypocrisy where people pretend to be more or better than they are. Too often, however, we see members of the Church who in their hearts know and believe, but through fear of public opinion fail to stand up and be counted. This kind of hypocrisy is as serious as the other; it makes it difficult for others to respect us, and often adversely affects or influences the lives of other members of the Church who expect us to stand by our commitments to the Church and not hesitate to manifest our faith.
>
> Only when we are seriously striving to live the teachings of Christ can we make any real spiritual progress. We must not fear, wherever we are, to live up to our convictions and to the standards of the Church. People, though they may criticize and ridicule, expect us to and respect us if we do. Living high standards cannot offend conscientious, fair-minded people. (In Conference Report, October 1970, pp. 52–53.)

I am still troubled by the words spoken to me by my high school basketball teammate: "I didn't even know you were a member of the Church." What a contrast my nonexample is to the exemplary courage demonstrated by young Joseph F. Smith on his return to Utah from his mission to the Hawaiian islands. As he was traveling through the western part of the country, having been away from home for nearly four years, he encountered a drunken mob of Mormon haters. Because of the persecution and the anti-Mormon sentiment in the region at the time it was extremely dangerous for Mormons to pass through that area. Young Joseph F. Smith had journeyed with a small party of wagons, and one day "a company of drunken men rode into the camp on horseback, cursing and swearing and threatening to kill any 'Mormons' that came within their path."

> It was the lot of Joseph F. Smith to meet these marauders first. Some of the brethren when they heard them coming had cautiously gone into the brush down the creek, out of sight where they waited for this band to pass. Joseph F. was a little distance from the camp gathering wood for the fire when these men rode up. When he saw them, he said, his first thought was to do what the other brethren had done, and seek shelter in the trees and in flight. Then the thought came to him, "Why should I run from these fellows?" With that thought in mind he boldly marched up with his arms full of wood to

> the campfire. As he was about to deposit his wood, one of the ruffians, still with his pistols in his hands and pointing at the youthful Elder, and cursing as only a drunken rascal can, declaring that it was his duty to exterminate every "Mormon" he should meet, demanded in a loud, angry voice, "Are you a 'Mormon'?"
>
> Without a moment of hesitation and looking the ruffian in the eye, Joseph F. Smith boldly answered, "Yes, siree; dyed in the wool; true blue, through and through."
>
> The answer was given boldly and without any sign of fear, which completely disarmed the belligerent man, and in his bewilderment, he grasped the missionary by the hand and said:
>
> "Well, you are the ——— ——— pleasantest man I ever met! Shake, young fellow. I am glad to see a man that stands up for his convictions."
>
> Joseph F. said in later years that he fully expected to receive the charge from this man's pistols, but he could take no other course even though it seemed that his death was to be the result. (Joseph Fielding Smith, *Life of Joseph F. Smith,* 2d ed. [Salt Lake City: Deseret Book Co., 1969], pp. 188–89.)

The courageous example of Joseph F. Smith reflects what the Apostle Paul declared to the Romans: "I am not ashamed of the gospel of Christ" (Romans 1:16). Sometimes some of us have the tendency to "hide in the bushes," spiritually speaking. We don't want to join up with the "drunken ruffians," but neither do we want to be "dyed in the wool; true blue, through and through." Being the kind of example the Savior expects of us may not always require us to verbally declare before the world our allegiance to the Lord, or to die as martyrs with the name of God on our lips, but it does require living our lives in such a way that our actions declare that we are not ashamed in any way of the Lord, his gospel, the Church, and the standards we have covenanted to obey.

The Powerful Influence of a Positive Example of Christlike Living

When my wife and family were waiting in the Tel Aviv airport for our return flight home to Utah, after living in Israel for a year (where I had the opportunity of teaching at the BYU Jerusalem Center), an interesting thing occurred that once again reminded me that we are always being watched. We were accompanying approximately 170 students who had been with us at the Jerusalem Center the previous semester. We were all really excited to go home, my family and myself included; and there was a lot of laughing and excited conversation. In fact, I felt the students were being a little too noisy and rambunctious—almost bordering on being obnoxious.

An Israeli gentleman sitting next to me in the waiting area spoke up and asked me, "Who are you people?" I was taken aback at first and was almost tempted to apologize for the noise of the students. Instead, I just told him that these young people were students from Brigham Young University who were returning to the USA after spending six months at the Jerusalem Center for Near Eastern Studies, and that I was one of their professors.

"You mean the Mormon university?" he asked. (It was always interesting to me that few in Israel, neither Arab nor Jew, knew anything about Brigham Young or had any idea of what or where Brigham Young University was. But it seemed that everyone in Jerusalem knew about the "Mormon university.")

"Yes," I responded, "we are all Mormons. Have you been to our Center?"

After telling me about his visit to what he characterized as "the most beautiful building in Jerusalem," he then observed, "I have been watching your group for a long time tonight. These are the most remarkable young people I have ever seen. They are so happy and clean-cut. They seem to just glow with goodness. What is it about you Mormons that makes you so different?"

Oh, how I wanted to answer his question, but I told him that one of the agreements that our church made to the Israeli government when we built our Center was that we would not proselyte in the land. That meant we would not even talk about our religion or answer questions about our beliefs. The man thought that was a "dumb idea" and said, "Israel is a free country; you ought to be able to talk about your religion to anyone." I told him that I took that commitment very seriously and when we give our word we keep it. "However," I joked, "I will gladly answer all of your questions and tell you what makes these kids 'glow with goodness' just as soon as we leave Israeli airspace."

Even in a busy, smoke-filled airport waiting area, with thousands of people from all over the world hurrying to catch their flights, we were noticed. The students weren't trying to "let [their] light so shine." It just did, because it radiated from within. We had many similar experiences throughout the land—some serious and some humorous.

Almost every time I led a group of students through the narrow, crowded streets of the Old City of Jerusalem, shopkeepers would greet us in their broken English: "You are Mormons! Come into my shop and I give you special Mormon discount." We would always laugh that they could spot us from a mile away, and we wondered what the "Mormon discount" really was. We didn't wear name tags or BYU baseball hats that would set us apart, but somehow we were different, and others recognized it. Although we couldn't talk about the Church or discuss the beliefs that made us so distinctive, we could still live our religion—and the power and influence of that example was felt by many.

On a field trip with my students to the ancient city of Beth Shean (it was called Scythopolis in Jesus' day), we had another experience that testified to us that not only is the light of righteousness seen by others, but they are also influenced thereby. As I was shepherding my class to the Roman theater where I was going to instruct them, my wife, Wendy, remained behind to direct any of the straggler students. As Wendy was walking over to the area where I was teaching the students, she overheard a gentleman say to a group of tourists, "Over there are students from Brigham Young University, the Mormon university. There is more virtue in that group of young people than anywhere else in the world." When one of the women in the group questioned him as to how he could say that, he responded simply, "Just look at them." Unbeknownst to the students, this interested group of tourists then came over near where my class was seated, and watched and listened as I taught them. They were as much, if not more, interested in seeing these young Latter-day Saints as they were in seeing the Roman ruins.

On another occasion when we took the students to Jordan,

we actually saw the fruits of Christlike example. At our sacrament meeting, held with the Amman Branch, one of the speakers bore testimony of how the example and spirit of the Mormon students visiting Jordan University from the Jerusalem Center the previous semester had led him to want to know about their church, "because there was something so good about them." (In Jordan, proselyting among Christians is allowed by law.) This young man, a Christian Arab, was so impressed with the BYU students that he sought out the Church in Amman, took the missionary lessons, and was baptized. In the audience at that sacrament meeting were many other Christian Arab students from Jordan University whose contact with our students had led them also to investigate the Church.

Numerous accounts and experiences similar to ours could be recited. There are tens of thousands of faithful Latter-day Saints in the Church today because of the powerful influence of Saints who, not consciously trying to be positive examples, and many times even without knowing they were being watched, reflected through their simple deeds, their kindness and love, and through their quiet acts of service the light and love of Christ that permeated their very souls. These modern exemplars, without any fanfare on their part, have let their "light so shine" that others have flocked to the Light and in turn have glorified their Father who is in heaven. The ripples of influence extend far beyond the individual who was first affected by their positive example.

One of the greatest examples of how a life that reflects the Savior can have untold influence is the Book of Mormon account of Ammon, a son of Mosiah. Through his example of righteousness, integrity, service, and faith, Ammon was able to share the gospel with King Lamoni. Not only was Lamoni led to the Light of the World through Ammon's light, but Lamoni's father was converted through the efforts of Ammon's brother Aaron "because of the generosity and the greatness of the words of thy brother Ammon" (Alma 22:3). "Out of small things proceedeth that which is great" (D&C 64:33). From the faithful example of Ammon came the conversion of the Lamanite nation (see Alma 22–26). Even today, we cannot underestimate the power that simple gospel-living—earnestly seeking to emulate the Great

Exemplar—can have in leading others to him. "By studying and living [the gospel's] principles and seeking the help of the Holy Ghost, any earnest seeker can know for himself that it is true," President Spencer W. Kimball testified. "But how much easier it is to understand and accept if the seeker after truth can also see the principles of the gospel at work in the lives of other believers. No greater service can be given to the missionary calling of this Church than to be exemplary in positive Christian virtues in our lives." (*The Teachings of Spencer W. Kimball,* ed. Edward L. Kimball [Salt Lake City: Bookcraft, 1982], p. 555.)

It is not just in the area of missionary work where a righteous example can have a positive influence. King Benjamin admonished his people, "If ye do not watch yourselves, and your thoughts, and your words, and your deeds, and observe the commandments of God, and continue in the faith . . . ye must perish" (Mosiah 4:30). This admonition is not just a warning of eternal consequences if we fail to do these things, but is also a reminder that everything we do affects ourselves and others right here and now.

Just as a bad example can influence other members of the Church in a negative way and lead them into sin, so can even a simple act that truly reflects the Savior help others to remember who they really are and inspire them to live the teachings of Christ they espouse. Elder John H. Groberg shared the following true story of a young Tongan boy during World War II that illustrates this principle:

> It was nighttime, but the moon and the stars gave Finau a feeling of assurance as he carefully guided his canoe across the wide expanse of the gently undulating Pacific Ocean. He constantly studied the stars, so he knew he was going in the right direction. The moon was up, and its brightness was only obscured by occasional wisps of high clouds.
>
> He had heard something about a "war" going on. Several of his friends had gone to the main island and traded their carved tikis and woven baskets to the American soldiers for money—more money than they had seen in all their 16 or so years of life. Finau had collected his very best baskets and carvings, and was already anticipating what he would do with the money he was sure to get from the Americans. . . .

The sun had just come up as he paddled his canoe through the reef opening and into the quiet lagoon. He saw an American soldier with a gun standing on the shore and made his course towards him. He had heard of guns and of the war and of the American soldiers and all the money they had and of all the things that money could buy. But now as he actually saw an American and observed his gun and realized he would have to talk to him, he became very nervous and uncertain of just what to do. Finau had learned a few words of English in his local school, but would it be enough? How much should he ask for his goods? He only knew pence and shillings and pounds, and he'd heard that the Americans used dimes and dollars. What were they worth? What would they buy? How should he begin?

Finau felt a little fear as he pulled his canoe up to the beach and the soldier came over. There was no one else on the beach. Would the soldier just take his goods? Would he shoot him? Uncertainty gripped his feelings as he climbed out of the canoe and pulled it onto the beach. He was here and he had traveled all night, so despite his fear he must go ahead.

"You buy?" he said to the soldier as he lifted a few baskets and tikis from the boat.

The young American soldier came over and looked at the items. "How much for this?" he asked, taking a beautifully carved tiki in his hand.

Finau almost panicked. He wasn't sure of the meaning of the strange words, but he felt he wanted him to say a price, so he blurted out, "Very good. Number one tiki. You buy. One pound."

The soldier looked quizzically at him, "You're new at this, aren't you? How about two dollars for the tiki and these three baskets?"

Finau wondered, "Is that enough? Maybe I should ask more and see what happens."

"Number one tiki, number one basket. Two dollars tiki, two dollars basket."

"Oh, you're a little bargainer are you? I'll tell you what. I've got a carton of cigarettes here. Cigarettes are worth more than money. I'll give you this whole carton for everything you have here. I guarantee you it's a good deal. They are good cigarettes. Here, I'll show you." The soldier lit one and took a puff and then offered it to Finau.

Up to now Finau had been uncertain of himself, but as he recognized the cigarettes and realized the intent of what was being said, he straightened up and firmly replied, "No!"

> "Oh, come on. One sale and you're all through. Think of the time you'll save, and if you don't want to smoke them all yourself you can trade them for other things—even money if you want. They're rationed, you know. Who can tell their value under these circumstances and in this faraway place? Come on, let's trade."
>
> "No," retorted Finau.
>
> "Come on, come on. What's the matter? I'll give them to you first, and you can unload your goods and leave them on the sand. You won't get a better deal." The soldier was noticeably irritated by this "stupid native's" refusal. He looked down at him with all the superiority he felt and again said, "Go ahead. It's okay. Cigarettes are valuable. Don't be so stupid."
>
> Finau, groping for words, stood erect and said, "No, me no smoke. Me Mormon."
>
> It was as though he had shot the young American. The soldier jerked in startled surprise. He carefully studied Finau, then looked past him and stared longingly into space. He looked again into the lowly native's eyes. He took the carton of cigarettes from under his arm, placed it in his right hand, crushed it, and heaved it far into the lagoon.
>
> Finau wondered, "Why?" He looked at the carton with its bobbing packages scattered about. Then he looked again at the soldier as he turned to walk away from the shore and heard him say, "Yeah, I know. So am I." ("You Never Know," *New Era,* March 1986, pp. 4–6.)

A true disciple of Christ, one who is seeking to emulate his perfect example, will always be an example because of the light that burns within—Christ's perfect light, which, like a city set on a hill, cannot be hid. If we have sought to internalize the teachings and love of the Savior and have partaken of his atoning sacrifice, we have his image graven upon our countenances. It is in this manner that the light that we put upon a candlestick for all to see is not us, however righteous we may be. It is Jesus who is the Light we must shine forth in our very being. The light we shine forth to the world, or our lives and our examples, is but a reflection of what we have allowed Christ, through our faith in him and our willingness to follow him, to do for us and to us. Just as the little girl in the airport surmised, from a simple act, the deep love a husband had for his wife, letting our light shine by seeking to follow the Savior in even simple ways will cause others to glorify God and observe, "You must really love him."

Christ also suffered for us,
leaving us an example,
that ye should follow his steps.
—1 Peter 2:21

2

Now I would that ye should remember that God has said that the inward vessel shall be cleansed first, and then shall the outer vessel be cleansed also.
—Alma 60:23

CLEANSING THE INNER VESSEL

Striving to Become Pure in Heart

After I proposed marriage to my sweetheart, Wendy, and she had agreed to commence her ultimate challenge and eternal "service project," we then embarked on the traditional diamond-engagement-ring-buying expedition. It was during this exciting endeavor that not only did I learn a lot about diamonds (and finances), but I also learned a valuable object lesson.

Perhaps everyone who has ever purchased a diamond has had an experience similar to ours. The jeweler took us to a back room that was equipped with what looked like an oversized microscope. He then took out several small padded envelopes, each containing one diamond. "Before you make such a significant purchase, you must be taught about the Cs of diamonds," he told us as he spread the envelopes out in front of us. From out of the first envelope he retrieved a large, spectacular-looking diamond. I immediately saw Wendy's eyes light up, and I got worried as I mistook the sparkle in her eyes for dollar signs. "This diamond isn't worth very much, and I wouldn't sell it to you," the jeweler said. "I have organized these diamonds according to their value." He pointed to the envelopes on the counter in front of us. "As you can see, this diamond is from the first envelope, meaning it is the least valuable." He could see the bewildered looks on our faces. "It may look impressive on the outside, but when you look at it closely on its inside through this magnification lens, you will clearly see all of its defects."

For the next several minutes Wendy and I received a jeweler's crash course about color, cut, clarity, and carat, and how each of these characteristics determine the value of a diamond. To the naked eye there were no differences among the diamonds except their size (carat), but when the salesman put other specimens under the diamond microscope I could clearly distinguish the different colors of diamonds, ranging from pristine white to a murkish yellow. The precision of the cut of the diamond was also visible. Some diamonds were cut so precisely that the lines of the cut seemed razor sharp, whereas others looked jagged or cracked. "The precision of the cut," the jeweler explained, "is what makes the diamond sparkle." I could see the clarity of different stones as well. Some were crystal clear, and others had dark inclusions inside the stone that ranged from large black spots to smaller defects that looked like squiggly lines. I never realized before that what the diamond was like on the inside was what primarily determined its real value.

Needless to say, I didn't buy the impressive-looking diamond that we were first shown. Perhaps I could have saved a lot of money, and maybe no one else would have known that inside that showy stone were deep, dark inclusions, a yucky yellow color, and craggy cuts; but I would have known. Instead I bought a diamond that didn't look all that impressive—it didn't weigh Wendy's hand down with its weight. It looked pretty average, but I knew, and Wendy knew, that this diamond got high grades when it came to color, cut, and clarity—those qualities that constituted real value.

Many times since that experience I have thought how much people are like diamonds. Some seem impressive on the outside, but inside they are full of all kinds of defects—some deep and dark. Some have devoted much of their time and energy to sanitizing their public persona by eliminating from their behavior the more obvious sins, but their inward attitudes and motivations have not received the same attention. I have thought how some may even be zirconium—they look like diamonds, but they aren't the real thing. Others that seem average or unimpressive are actually of highest quality; the intents of their hearts are pure and their inward goodness blesses all around them. For these good people, what you see is what you get. There are no deep, dark defects hiding from public view like skeletons in the closet.

In the Sermon on the Mount, Jesus taught his disciples that they must go beyond just the outward expressions of gospel living and seek a higher righteousness by purifying the inward man. He criticized the scribes and Pharisees on two accounts: First, they were obsessed with mere compliance with the outward ordinances and performances of the Mosiac law as well as the traditions of the elders, yet they overlooked the inward spiritual intent of the law. Second, and worse, they were hypocritical; they pretended to be one thing on the outside but were just the opposite on the inside.

> For I say unto you, That except your righteousness shall exceed the righteousness of the scribes and Pharisees, ye shall in no case enter into the kingdom of heaven.
>
> Ye have heard that it was said by them of old time, Thou shalt not kill; and whosoever shall kill shall be in danger of the judgment:
>
> But I say unto you, That whosoever is angry with his brother without a cause shall be in danger of the judgment: and whosoever shall say to his brother, Raca, shall be in danger of the council: but whosoever shall say, Thou fool, shall be in danger of hell fire. . . .
>
> Ye have heard that it was said by them of old time, Thou shalt not commit adultery:
>
> But I say unto you, That whosoever looketh on a woman to lust after her hath committed adultery with her already in his heart. . . .
>
> Ye have heard that it hath been said, An eye for an eye, and a tooth for a tooth:
>
> But I say unto you, That ye resist not evil: but whosoever shall smite thee on thy right cheek, turn to him the other also.
>
> And if any man will sue thee at the law, and take away thy coat, let him have thy cloke also.
>
> And whosoever shall compel thee to go a mile, go with him twain. . . .

> Ye have heard that it hath been said, Thou shalt love thy neighbour, and hate thine enemy.
>
> But I say unto you, Love your enemies, bless them that curse you, do good to them that hate you, and pray for them which despitefully use you, and persecute you. . . .
>
> For if ye love them which love you, what reward have ye? do not even the publicans the same?
>
> And if ye salute your brethren only, what do ye more than others? do not even the publicans so? (Matthew 5:20–22, 27–28, 38–41, 43–44, 46–47.)

Responding to Jesus' Call to a Higher Righteousness

In this sermon Jesus taught his disciples that it was not enough, spiritually speaking, to merely keep the stipulations of the law of Moses and the carnal commandments, for even the people who were hypocritical and superficial did that. Righteousness—being Christlike—requires proper intentions and attitudes as well as proper behavior. Jesus' use of the phrase "but I say unto you" was an invitation to go beyond the letter of the law to the spirit of the law. He was urging us to get past mere avoidance of wickedness that is outwardly visible. He was inviting us to become righteous, which requires the *internalization* of gospel principles and may not be fully observed and rightly evaluated by others. Being more Christlike requires not only a change in our outward behaviors but also a change in our heart, might, and mind as well.

It is harder to be Christlike than just mindlessly obedient. As Frederic W. Farrar insightfully penned:

> It is easy to be a slave to the letter, and difficult to enter into the spirit; easy to obey a number of outward rules, difficult to enter intelligently and self-sacrificingly into the will of God; easy to entangle the soul in a network of petty observances, difficult to yield the obedience of an enlightened heart; easy to be haughtily exclusive, difficult to be humbly spiritual; easy to be an ascetic or a formalist, difficult to be pure, and loving, and wise, and free; easy to be a Pharisee, difficult to be a disciple; very easy to embrace a self-satisfying and

> sanctimonious system of rabbinical observances, very difficult to love God with all the heart, and all the might, and all the soul, and all the strength. (*The Life of Christ* [1875; reprint, Salt Lake City: Bookcraft, 1994], p. 445.)

To the hypocritical scribes and Pharisees, Jesus declared: "Cleanse first that which is within the cup and platter, that the outside of them may be clean also" (Matthew 23:26). Following Christ to this higher level of righteousness requires the purifying of the inward man; then righteous outward behaviors will naturally follow. Becoming like Christ sounds like an overwhelming, daunting, almost impossible task, at least to me. How can I do this? For me, the only way it can be done is like the proverbial eating of an elephant—one bite at a time. I have found that focusing on the little things makes the big things fall into their proper places. I think it was for this very reason that Jesus beckoned his disciples to real righteousness, not just compliance with the law; for if they were truly righteous they would also be obedient to the requirements of the gospel.

"Thou Shalt Not Get Angry"

Ye have heard that it was said by them of old time,
Thou shalt not kill; and whosoever shall kill
shall be in danger of the judgment:
But I say unto you, That whosoever is angry with his brother
without a cause shall be in danger of the judgment:
and whosoever shall say to his brother, Raca,
shall be in danger of the council:
but whosoever shall say, Thou fool,
shall be in danger of hell fire.
—Matthew 5:21–22

In all my years in the Church I can't remember one talk given in a sacrament or priesthood meeting or any other kind of meeting on why we shouldn't commit murder. I must admit that we have never had a family home evening lesson on murder either. I think both my family and I pretty well understand that concept.

When it comes to "Thou shalt not kill," I think I'm pretty good at living that commandment—but maybe that's not saying much.

In contrast, I have heard numerous talks and lessons on abuse, contention, backbiting, fighting, and other related issues. It seems to me that in the Sermon on the Mount, Jesus is teaching us that control of anger and thoughts must precede any lasting control of behavior. It seems that Jesus was saying then and now, "If you just avoid killing someone, or abusing or hurting another, you may be doing a good thing, but you are living a lesser law. But if you can master your emotions so that you are no longer quick to anger, then you are living the higher law." It is more difficult, yet yields even greater spiritual returns, to control the inward man than to just exercise self-control regarding outward behaviors. In a general priesthood meeting President Ezra Taft Benson declared, "If a man does not control his temper, it is a sad admission that he is not in control of his thoughts. He then becomes a victim of his own passions and emotions, which lead him to actions that are totally unfit for civilized behavior, let alone behavior for a priesthood holder." (In Conference Report, October 1986, p. 62.) A person who never seeks to control the inward emotion of anger may never fully be free of abuse, contention, and unkindness. He may not act out these behaviors, but they are still in his heart and are part of his character.

It is a good thing for me not to hit my wife if I am angry with her, but seething in anger and unkind feelings not only is destructive to our relationship; it also cankers my own soul and stifles spirituality, because the Spirit of the Lord cannot dwell in an angry heart. President David O. McKay taught, "Anger itself does [a person] more harm than the condition which aroused his anger, and in reality, . . . he suffers more from the vexation than he does from the acts that aroused that vexation. I wonder how long it will take us to realize that in matters of temper nothing can bring us damage but ourselves." (*Something Higher Than Self,* Brigham Young University Speeches of the Year [Provo, Utah, 12 October 1965].)

I am an avid sports fan. In fact, in my younger years I was a pretty good athlete. (I know that may be as hard for you to believe as it is for my children. I have discovered that when it comes to the athletic prowess of my youth, the older I become, the better I was.) It didn't take me long to realize that anger or a bad temper adversely affected me as an athlete, whether I was playing basketball or baseball. Although some excuse their anger or temper in athletics by calling it "competitiveness," to me there is a difference. If I lost my cool, my playing ability actually declined. Anger retarded my athletic skills. Control and concentration enhanced those skills. I was only able to play to the best of my ability when I was in control of my emotions. When I realized that, I worked hard to eliminate anger from my game.

I have also experienced the detrimental effects of anger as a fan. There is a standing joke in our family when I am watching a BYU basketball or football game on TV: "Get out of the house if the Cougars are losing." I have been known to shout in disgust, huff and puff, throw things, and so on. But I have learned that my anger or my outbursts have never helped the Cougars to play better or the officials to see better. It only makes me miserable, and when I am in an angry mood, it also affects my family. They don't like to be around me when BYU loses. We can laugh about it, but it vividly illustrates the futility of anger. It really does not help anybody or anything. The principles are the same whether it be in sports or family relationships—anger adversely affects us, diminishes our much-needed skills, and alienates others.

Seeking to emulate Jesus' higher righteousness requires control at first, then ultimately the elimination of anger. If anger is eliminated from the heart, abusive outbursts, verbal as well as physical, will disappear. If I can control my thoughts and feelings of anger, my spirit will be free from the seething of anger that poisons my own soul and precludes the spirit of love and peace from prevailing. Cleansing the heart of anger naturally leads to more Christlike kindness and inner peace.

"Thou Shalt Not Lust"

Ye have heard that it was said by them of old time,
Thou shalt not commit adultery:
But I say unto you, That whosoever looketh on a woman
to lust after her hath committed adultery
with her already in his heart.
—Matthew 5:27–28

When I was being interviewed for my mission by my stake president, he illustrated the Savior's concept of higher righteousness as it pertains to moral cleanliness. I had been interviewed by my bishop and had been asked the question "Are you morally clean?" scores of times previous to this momentous interview. I had always been taught that if I had not engaged in certain sexual activities (or properly repented of such transgressions if I had), I could answer in the affirmative to the question of moral worthiness.

"Are you morally clean?" the stake president asked me as expected. "Before you answer," he continued, "let me teach you what I mean by that question." For the next several minutes President Ahlstrom taught me, in such a manner that I could not misunderstand, that moral cleanliness not only involved the avoidance of outward behaviors but also the control and elimination of inward thoughts and desires that were unworthy and unbecoming of an ambassador of the Lord. He explained that virtue is what a person *is* as much as what one *does*—that a person could be unworthy or unvirtuous even without committing certain immoral actions. At the conclusion of this teaching moment, President Ahlstrom then asked again, "Are you morally clean?" This powerful interview was as much instructive as evaluative. I now had a clearer understanding of the higher righteousness Jesus desired. I have thought of this interview many times through years when I was asked as a teacher, "How far is too far?" or when I, as a bishop, have asked ward members, "Are you morally clean?"

The natural man, one who lives a telestial law, engages in both immoral behaviors and immoral thoughts. A person who seeks to live a higher law but only a terrestrial law is concerned solely with behavior. They would never actually commit adultery or engage in any related behaviors, but they have no qualms about entertaining immoral thoughts and fantasies. When they hear the phrase "moral cleanliness," they think only of the avoidance of such practices as adultery and fornication. Such chastity is not virtue. It is the higher righteousness—virtue, not mere abstinence—that Jesus calls us to. The Christlike standard of moral purity requires us to "let virtue garnish [our] thoughts unceasingly" (D&C 121:45).

Several years ago, while I was serving as a bishop, I was taught a valuable lesson from a ward member during the course of a temple recommend interview. After I had asked all of the standard questions, I inquired of him if there was anything that was bothering him that he would like to talk about with me.

"I have a hard time controlling my thoughts sometimes," he responded. "When it is hot outside and I notice a lot of the young women in the area wearing immodest clothes, it is really hard for me to keep unworthy thoughts out of my mind."

My first reaction (the natural man in me) was to say, "Welcome to the real world. That's just part of living, especially in this day and age. It will be a constant battle." I suppose I was more inspired at that moment, and instead of just blurting out my natural-man beliefs, I asked him, "How are you dealing with this challenge?"

Almost apologetically he explained to me that he wasn't very good at controlling his thoughts, so he had decided instead to control his environment. He explained that he had come to the conclusion that he couldn't go to the popular waterpark because of all of the young women in immodest swimsuits. He spoke of other environmental controls he had imposed upon himself. He thought of himself as weak and lacking self-control, but the more I listened and thought about what he was saying, the more I viewed him as smart, strong, and more in control than others who think they can control their thoughts regardless of the environment.

I have discovered that most of us equate controlling our thoughts with singing a hymn. While I believe in and have used that tactic to deal with unwanted, involuntary unworthy thoughts, I am convinced that by itself, singing a hymn is not a panacea that will cause us to come off victorious against all unworthy and lustful thoughts. Let me illustrate what I mean by this with an exaggerated example that I use with my students. "How would you feel about a man taking his hymnbook to an XXX-rated movie theater?" I ask my students. "Will his lustful thoughts be eliminated with his singing? What if he sings really loud?" Usually the students laugh and get the point. Singing a hymn—whatever the hymn, however loud we sing, and however many times we repeat it—will not counteract our own wilful exposure to those influences and media that are by their very nature designed to produce lustful thoughts and desires. It is one thing to have garbage thrown at us, which we can wash off as quickly as we can. It is quite another thing to *choose* to eat the garbage. I have learned that controlling our thoughts requires controlling our own will as well as our environment. Like the adage states, "You are what you eat." We cannot "eat" that which is defiled and impure without becoming defiled ourselves and ultimately spiritually sick.

An Education Week speaker shared a thought with me many years ago that I believe to be not only insightful but practical. He explained that when he goes to the temple or to sacrament meeting and renews covenants, he makes a "sub-covenant" of something he needs to work on that will help him to more fully live the spirit of the overall principle. For example, when he covenants to be morally clean, he might promise the Lord that not only will he not commit adultery but he will do some specific thing that shows that he will not even have immorality in his heart or his head. Such sub-covenants are really a wilful, conscientious effort to protect the moral environment of his life and the loyalty of his heart.

The Savior did not issue his higher law to his disciples merely to safeguard their behavior, or to prevent them from crossing over the line from mental adultery to the actual adulterous deed. He wanted them to become more like him—to be virtuous people, not just non-adulterers. As the ancient proverb reminds us, "For as he thinketh in his heart, so is he" (Proverbs 23:7). Seeking to follow after Jesus' higher righteousness not only affects our behavior, it changes our very being, for we are what we think. President George Albert Smith related the following:

> As a child, thirteen years of age, I went to school at the Brigham Young Academy. It was fortunate that part of my instruction came under Dr. Karl G. Maeser. . . . Dr. Maeser one day stood up and said:
>
> "Not only will you be held accountable for the things you do, but you will be held responsible for the very thoughts you think."
>
> . . . [Later] it suddenly came to me what he meant . . . : Why of course you will be held accountable for your thoughts, because when your life is completed in mortality, it will be the sum of your thoughts. That one suggestion has been a great blessing to me all

my life, and it has enabled me upon many occasions to avoid thinking improperly, because I realize that I will be, when my life's labor is complete, the product of my thoughts. (*Sharing the Gospel with Others,* comp. Preston Nibley [Salt Lake City: Deseret Book Co., 1948], pp. 62–63.)

"Thou Shalt Love and Forgive Your Enemies"

Ye have heard that it hath been said,
Thou shalt love thy neighbour, and hate thine enemy.
But I say unto you, Love your enemies,
bless them that curse you, do good to them that hate you,
and pray for them which despitefully use you, and persecute you.
—Matthew 5:43–44

As Jesus taught his disciples anciently in the Sermon on the Mount, it is easy to love those who love us. It is no great challenge to be friends with those who are already our friends. Even the wicked do this much, but the Savior demands a higher righteousness—that we love those who do not love us and forgive those who have offended or deeply hurt us. This is a real test of our discipleship. Even the Apostle Peter found the Savior's charge more difficult than he imagined. "How oft shall my brother sin against me, and I forgive him? till seven times?" he asked the Master (Matthew 18:21). It is evident from Peter's inquiry that he had a limited understanding of the higher law Jesus expects his disciples to live. To a large degree this deficiency was due to the Mosaic law's teachings on "an eye for an eye" retribution. Peter's follow-up question "Till seven times?" was intended to be a generous gesture that went beyond the requirement of the ancient law. Jesus taught the higher law once again when he responded to Peter, "I say not unto thee, Until seven times: but, Until seventy times seven" (Matthew 18:22). Certainly the Lord was not saying we must only forgive 490 times, but rather that we must forgive others continually. "For if ye forgive men their trespasses, your heavenly Father will also forgive you: but if ye forgive not men their trespasses, neither will your Father forgive your trespasses" (Matthew 6:14–15).

In our dispensation the Lord reiterated this higher law when he declared to the Prophet Joseph Smith:

> My disciples, in days of old, sought occasion against one another and forgave not one another *in their hearts;* and for this evil they were afflicted and sorely chastened.
>
> Wherefore, I say unto you, that ye ought to forgive one another; for that forgiveth not his brother his trespasses standeth condemned before the Lord; for there remaineth in him the greater sin.
>
> I, the Lord will forgive whom I will forgive, but of you it is required to forgive all men.
>
> And ye ought to say *in your hearts*—let God judge between me and thee, and reward thee according to thy deeds. (D&C 64:8–11; emphasis added.)

Perhaps the most important words in the foregoing revelation are the oft-overlooked phrases "in their hearts" and "in your hearts." Loving and forgiving one's enemies must emanate from the heart. If our hearts are not purified of all ill will, no outward gesture of reconciliation will have any meaning. I learned from personal experience that there is a huge difference between the lip service I give to the principle of forgiving others and really forgiving in my heart.

Several years ago someone trespassed against a member of my family and thus offended me in turn. I held a grudge and found myself disliking this person immensely. Recognizing that I was harboring ill feelings and that I needed to forgive and forget, I made halfhearted efforts to do things that could be perceived as forgiveness. I spoke to the person at church, treated him nicely, and acted as though there was nothing wrong between us. I even gave the offender things that were important to me (I guess I viewed these gifts as peace offerings). I soon discovered that instead of feeling better, I was actually feeling worse—more resentful and bitter. The cankering of my soul continued. Even though I was making token gestures of forgiveness, I was not yet willing to forgive in my heart. What must I do to move from the outward appearances of loving and forgiving my enemies to actually doing so inwardly? The answer to my soul-felt inquiry was found in the very words of the Savior: "But I say unto you, Love your enemies, bless them that curse you, do good to them that hate you, and pray for them which despitefully use you, and persecute you" (Matthew 5:44). The words the Master used—love, bless, do good, pray—imply actions that we choose to do rather than feelings that we naturally feel. The Savior's celestial charge is based not on emotion but on volition. I can choose to forgive and forget. I may not be able to cognitively forget how I was wronged or by whom, but I can forget in the sense that I can conscientiously commit or covenant to let go of my hard feelings. I can wilfully choose to no longer dwell on the wrongs done me and I can wilfully force thoughts of retribution out of my mind. I can choose to leave it alone.

Similarly, loving my enemies may not involve liking them or their deeds. I may not be required to do some magnanimous gesture to outwardly prove that I love my enemies, but I can remember and practice the Golden Rule with all people, especially those who have harmed me. C. S. Lewis perhaps explained it best:

> We must try to feel about the enemy as we feel about ourselves—to wish that he were not bad, to hope that he may, in this world or another, be cured: in fact, to wish his good. That is what is meant in the Bible by loving him: wishing his good, not feeling fond of him nor saying he is nice when he is not. . . .
>
> . . . The rule for all of us is perfectly simple. Do not waste time bothering whether you "love" your neighbour; act as if you did. As soon as we do this we find one of the great secrets. When you are behaving as if you loved someone, you will presently come to love him. . . . If you do him a good turn, you will find yourself disliking him less. . . .
>
> . . . The difference between a Christian and a worldly man is not that the worldly man has only affections or "likings" and the Christian has only "charity." The worldly man treats people kindly because he "likes" them: the Christian, trying to treat every one kindly, finds himself liking more and more people as he goes on—including people he could not even have imagined himself liking at the beginning. (*Mere Christianity* [New York: Macmillan, 1960], pp. 108, 116–18.)

As we seek to let go of all bitterness and put pettiness behind us, as we do good to and pray for those who have offended or injured us, we must also plead with our Heavenly Father to fill our hearts with the spirit of forgiveness. I can seek to do my part to live the higher law, but ultimately it is the Lord who can change my heart. "If there be any within the sound of my voice who nurture in their hearts the poisonous brew of enmity toward another, I plead with you to ask the Lord for strength to forgive," declared Elder Gordon B. Hinckley. "It may not be easy, and it may not come quickly. But if you will seek it with sincerity and cultivate it, it *will* come. . . . There will come into your heart a peace otherwise unattainable." (In Conference Report, October 1980, p. 87; emphasis in original.)

Doing the Right Things for the Right Reasons

Like diamonds that look impressive on the outside but are dark and flawed on the inside, the scribes and Pharisees were condemned by the Savior for their hypocrisy. "Woe unto you, scribes and Pharisees, hypocrites!" Jesus declared. "For ye are like unto whited sepulchres, which indeed appear beautiful outward, but are within full of dead men's bones, and of all uncleanness. Even so ye also outwardly appear righteous unto men, but within ye are full of hypocrisy and iniquity." (Matthew 23:27–28.) The Greek word from which the word *hypocrite* was translated literally means "to act," like playing a character role in a play. We are all familiar with hypocrisy. We see blatant examples of it all around us from people who don't "practice what they preach." They are like zirconium stones passing themselves off as costly diamonds. The hypocrisy Jesus is condemning in the Sermon on the Mount, however, is somewhat different. It is a subtle yet insidious form of hypocrisy that is almost unrecognizable, but if not eradicated it fatally flaws the human heart. Jesus' rebuke of these hypocrites may actually have seemed ironic, for he was condemning the most religious, the most observant, and those whom many considered the very role models of devout Judaism. They were doing all the right things on the outside, such as fasting, praying, serving in leadership positions, and contributing alms for the poor. It was not so much *what* these people were doing that Jesus decried as it was *why* they were doing what they were doing. It was the inner motivation for their "righteous acts" that Jesus questioned.

Motivations and intentions speak loudly about who it is we really love and desire to serve and from whom we desire approbation:

> Take heed that ye do not your alms before men, to be seen of them: otherwise ye have no reward of your Father which is in heaven.
>
> Therefore when thou doest thine alms, do not sound a trumpet before thee, as the hypocrites do in the synagogues and in the streets, that they may have glory of men. Verily I say unto you, They have their reward.
>
> But when thou doest alms, let not thy left hand know what thy right hand doeth:
>
> That thine alms may be in secret: and thy Father which seeth in secret himself shall reward thee openly.
>
> And when thou prayest, thou shalt not be as the hypocrites are: for they love to pray standing in the synagogues and in the corners of the streets, that they may be seen of men. Verily I say unto you, They have their reward.
>
> But thou, when thou prayest, enter into thy closet, and when thou has shut thy door, pray to thy Father which is in secret; and thy Father which seeth in secret shall reward thee openly.
>
> But when ye pray, use not vain repetitions, as the heathen do: for they think that they shall be heard for their much speaking.
>
> Be not therefore like unto them: for your Father knoweth what things ye have need of, before ye ask him. . . .
>
> Moreover when ye fast, be not, as the hypocrites, of a sad countenance: for they disfigure their faces, that they may appear unto men to fast. Verily I say unto you, they have their reward.
>
> But thou, when thou fastest, anoint thine head, and wash thy face;
>
> That thou appear not unto men to fast, but unto thy Father which is in secret: and thy Father which seeth in secret, shall reward thee openly. (Matthew 6:1–8, 16–18.)

Jesus' opening caution to "take heed" seems to imply that it is a universal tendency of the natural man to seek recognition, honors, and acceptance from others. The Prophet Joseph explained that "there are many called, but few are chosen" because "their hearts are set so much upon the things of this world, and aspire to the honors of men" (D&C 121:34–35). He confirmed that it is the "nature and disposition of almost all men" to seek "to gratify [their] pride, [their] vain ambition," and when one gets a little authority, to "exercise unrighteous dominion" (D&C 121:37, 39). Jesus urges his disciples, both ancient and modern, to overcome the natural man and be more like him by doing the right things for the right reasons. "We must not only *do* what is right. We must act for the right reasons," Elder Dallin H. Oaks wrote. "It is easier to have clean hands than to have a pure heart. It is easier to control our acts than to control our thoughts. The requirement that our good acts must be accompanied by good motives is subtle and difficult in practice." (*Pure in Heart* [Salt Lake City: Bookcraft, 1988], pp. 15, 18.)

Just as the scribes and Pharisees did good and noble acts not out of their love for God but primarily to be seen of men, there is an almost universal temptation for us in the Church today to unwittingly do the same. While I cannot judge the motivations and intents of others, I know my own weaknesses. Therefore, I am left wondering and worrying about the motivation behind what I see sometimes among the Saints and in my own service in the kingdom. When Jesus announced to the Apostles at the Last Supper that one among them would betray him, instead of pointing accusing fingers (I think they knew within themselves who the betrayer was) they each asked the Master, "Is it I?" (See Mark 14:19.) It is this type of personal introspection that is needed in the quest to become more Christlike. As I seek to "cleanse the inner vessel" and examine not only the thoughts and feelings in my heart but also the motives for my actions, it would be beneficial to consider the following question: "Why am I doing this?" Elder Oaks has written that this question should be a guidepost for us along the path of discipleship: "We can work to reform our motives if we are continually asking ourselves: Why am I taking this action? That question is especially important for actions that we suppose to be good. It reminds us that it is not enough to act in ways that seem to be good. We must act for the right reasons. If we truly desire to please God and serve him, continual self-examination of our reasons for actions cannot fail to expose our selfish and sordid motives and challenge us to reform them." (*Pure in Heart,* p. 148.)

This "continual self-examination" advocated by Elder Oaks may be as painful as it is instructive. It can and should be applied to a myriad of practical everyday situations we find ourselves in. I have struggled with the question "Why am I doing this?" in numerous circumstances and settings. Such difficult self-examination may include many, if not all, of the following real-life questions:

—Are my comments in church meetings motivated out of a sincere hungering and thirsting after gospel knowledge and a humble desire to contribute to others' understanding, or are they more to show off how much I know or to set straight the comments of someone else?
—Do I seek to outdo others in my Church calling? Do I feel some sense of competition or comparison with others?
—When I share personal spiritual experiences, am I doing so under the influence and prompting of the Spirit for the edification of others, or am I trying to impress people with how "spiritual" I am?
—Do I bear my testimony in testimony meeting out of a spiritual desire to praise God and testify of those sacred truths that have been revealed, or am I using it as a forum to impress others?
—Is my service in the Church dependent upon being in "high-profile" positions, or would I still faithfully magnify my calling if I was serving where no one else would see or notice my efforts?
—Do I feel a pang of envy when others receive certain callings or receive awards or recognitions?
—Do I need and am I motivated more by the praises of men than by the quiet assurance that the Lord is mindful and accepting of my efforts?
—Do I find myself concerned about maintaining my public

image or Church image? Do I seek to control my children because their behavior may adversely affect my image?
—Is my service more anonymous and unheralded than mere involvement in organized ward or quorum service projects?

Some of these questions are extremely difficult to answer, and often there is a fine line between altruistic and self-serving behavior. I believe that is the very point Jesus is making by his call to a higher righteousness. The hypocrisy of doing the right things out of impure motives—to be seen of men and for the praises of men—infects our soul, however slowly and subtly. We must continually assess our motives and priorities. We must seek to be perfectly honest with ourselves regarding our true motivations. Becoming more Christlike requires not only a purification of *what* I do, but also *why* I do it. "For behold, God hath said a man being evil cannot do that which is good," the prophet Mormon taught, "for if he offereth a gift [or performs a righteous act], . . . except he shall do it with real intent it profiteth him nothing. For behold, it is not counted unto him for righteousness." (Moroni 7:6–7.) We cannot truly follow Christ with supposedly good actions that are perfomed for the wrong reasons, out of an impure heart. The Lord has given us the right reason that should guide all our actions and service: "Every man seeking the interest of his neighbor, and doing all things with an eye single to the glory of God" (D&C 82:19).

Cleanse first that which is within the cup and platter,
that the outside of them may be clean also.
—Matthew 23:26

Jesus is beckoning us to become more like him inwardly as well as outwardly. He wants us to be like diamonds that sparkle to the naked eye and are pure within as well. He beckons us to change not only our actions but also our attitudes. He desires from us not only clean hands but also pure hearts. "If we do righteous acts and refrain from evil acts, we have clean hands," taught Elder Oaks. "If we act for the right motives and if we refrain from forbidden desires and attitudes, we have pure hearts." (*Pure in Heart,* p. 1.)

Who shall ascend into the hill of the Lord?
or who shall stand in his holy place?
He that hath clean hands, and a pure heart;
who hath not lifted up his soul unto vanity, nor sworn deceitfully.
He shall receive the blessing from the Lord,
and righteousness from the God of his salvation.
—Psalm 24:3–5

3

I beseech you therefore, brethren,
by the mercies of God, that ye present
your bodies a living sacrifice, holy,
acceptable unto God, which is your
reasonable service.
—Romans 12:1

Living for the Lord

Taking Up the Cross Through Daily Sacrifice

As I loaded my suitcases into the trunk of the car, the reality of my lifelong goal started to sink in. I had been called to serve a full-time mission to Denmark, the land of my ancestors. I was excited and anxious to begin my service, but as I drove with my parents to Salt Lake City to enter the mission home, I began to feel fear.

After many miles of silence, my father sensed that something was wrong and asked what was troubling me. I said that I was nervous (I wasn't about to admit that I was actually scared to death)—nervous about learning a new language, nervous about whether I would be a good missionary, nervous about leaving behind family and friends. At that point in my life, two years seemed not quite an eternity, but close.

There was a commingling of thoughts and emotions not only in my own mind and heart but also in my parents'. While I can't remember exactly what my dad said in my pre-mission pep talk, I do remember an example that he used. "It's quite natural for you to have some feelings of apprehension," he reassured me. "You're having to sacrifice some things to do other things. And it is normal to have some fear of the unknown. Imagine how your grandfather must have felt when he left his family and friends behind to come to America."

My father then recounted once again to me how my grandfather had left behind the family farm in Denmark to come to America, the land of promise and opportunity. With virtually no money or earthly possessions, and not knowing a single word of English, he traveled by ship to New York. He then worked odd jobs from New York City to the stockyards of Chicago to save enough money to come to Idaho, where he could homestead land. "Granddad Top," as he was always known to us, lived in a dugout house in the ground while he farmed the land and saved enough money to build an aboveground house suitable for a family. After two years he then returned to Denmark, not to stay in the comforts of his homeland but to take his wife back to America to the home he had established in the harsh southeastern Idaho environment.

I have thought many times of my grandfather's sacrifice and hard work, but I am even more touched by the sacrifice of my grandmother, who died long before I was born. She left a large, loving family and a beautiful farm in the lush landscape of Denmark to follow my grandfather to a truly foreign land and a very difficult life. Although she longed to return to her beloved Denmark, she never again saw the home and family she left behind.

There were many times on my mission when I wondered why I was there, because so few wanted to hear my message—so many doors were slammed in my face, so many rejections, so much discouragement. In my darkest moments when I wondered if my sacrifices had any meaning, I would think of my Danish grandparents, who had sacrificed so much to come to America. Because of their settling in that part of Idaho, my father was later introduced to the gospel and ultimately joined the Church. To a large degree, the myriad blessings springing forth from the gospel that have blessed me and and my family resulted from the sacrifices of those courageous grandparents. Over a half-century later, my sacrifices to serve as a missionary in their beloved Denmark may not have resulted in many baptisms, but it was a small way to show my appreciation for and bring honor to my Danish pioneer grandparents.

There are thousands upon thousands of similar stories of people who have sacrificed virtually everything they had, including their own lives, for the sake of the gospel. The history of the Church and numerous family histories are laced with such accounts, each an integral piece in the expansive saga of sacrifice among the Lord's people. This spiritual saga reflects the spirit of the Savior's injunction: "He that loveth father or mother more than me is not worthy of me: and he that loveth son or daughter more than me is not worthy of me. And he that taketh not his cross, and followeth after me, is not worthy of me." (Matthew 10:37–38.) To follow Christ and to be a determined disciple requires a faith and commitment that comes only from a willingness to lay one's all on the altar of God. The Prophet Joseph Smith declared:

> For a man to lay down his all, his character and reputation, his honor, and applause, his good name among men, his houses, his lands, his brothers and sisters, his wife and children, and even his own life also . . . requires more than mere belief or supposition that he is doing the will of God; but actual knowledge, realizing that, when these sufferings are ended, he will enter into eternal rest, and be a partaker of the glory of God. . . .
>
> . . . A religion that does not require the sacrifice of all things never has power sufficient to produce the faith necessary unto life and salvation; for, from the first existence of man, the faith necessary unto the enjoyment of life and salvation never could be obtained without the sacrifice of all earthly things. It was through this sacrifice, and this only, that God has ordained that men should enjoy eternal life. (In *Lectures on Faith* 6:5, 7.)

We read in the scriptures and in the annals of Church history of men and women who possessed this very kind of faith—faith they obtained through sacrifice. I think of Abraham's near-sacrifice of Isaac (see Genesis 22:12, 16–17) and of Peter and Andrew, who, when called by Jesus, "straightway left their nets, and followed him" (Matthew 4:20). I am sobered by the sacrifices of our pioneer forefathers who were persecuted and driven from their homes and then willingly left behind a prosperous Nauvoo, forsaking comfortable homes and productive farms and businesses, to undertake the uncertain and dangerous trek to the Rocky mountains.

Stillman Pond was one of those early pioneers who made tremendous personal sacrifices for the gospel's sake. His poignant story has always been a source of inspiration to me. Stillman Pond was a prosperous Nauvoo merchant at the time of the exodus of the Latter-day Saints from Nauvoo. Sick with fever, he was too weak to drive his team. He lay in the back of the wagon and his wife drove the wagon westward with their six children. Two other children, as well as a set of baby twins, had contracted malaria during the epidemic that plagued the Saints when they first settled in the swampland destined to become "Nauvoo the beautiful."

They had died and were buried in Nauvoo. The winter of 1846–47 took a terrible toll on Stillman Pond. His family had come down with the same serious illness that had threatened his life. On December 2 his fourteen-year-old daughter, Laura Jane Pond, died of "chills and fever." Two days later, Harriet, an eleven-year-old daughter, died of the same illness. On December 7 Abigail A. Pond, age eighteen, died of "chills and fever"—three children dead and buried all within the space of just a few days. The trial of his faith, however, was far from over. Slightly more than a month later, his six-year-old son, Lyman, died. His supreme sacrifice, his "Abrahamic test" in the cause of faith, was yet to come: In May of 1847 his beloved wife, Maria, died and was buried on the plains. With two surviving children, he moved on.

Even after having paid such a costly price to follow the Church to the West, Stillman Pond was yet to be called upon to sacrifice even more for the kingdom of God. After having settled in the Salt Lake Valley, he, like so many other pioneers who had sacrificed so much to "find the place which God for us prepared, far away in the West" ("Come, Come, Ye Saints," in *Hymns,* no. 30), was called by the prophet to once again uproot his family and colonize other areas of the Great Basin. Despite the hardships and heartaches, the uspeakable grief, the inconveniences and sacrifice, Stillman Pond remained true and steadfast, his faith strengthened and his life sanctified through sacrifice.

What a contrast the rich young ruler in the book of Luke is to Stillman Pond, father Abraham, and thousands of others who have made supreme sacrifices in the cause of truth and righteousness.

> And a certain ruler asked him, saying, Good Master, what shall I do to inherit eternal life?
>
> And Jesus said unto him, Why callest thou me good? none is good, save one, that is, God.
>
> Thou knowest the commandments, Do not commit adultery, Do not kill, Do not steal, Do not bear false witness, Honour thy father and thy mother.
>
> And he said, All these have I kept from my youth up.
>
> Now when Jesus heard these things, he said unto him, Yet lackest thou one thing: sell all that thou hast, and distribute unto the poor, and thou shalt have treasure in heaven: and come, follow me.
>
> And when he heard this, he was very sorrowful: for he was very rich. (Luke 18:18–23.)

Even though this rich young man had been keeping the commandments from the time of his youth, he disappears from the scene, never appearing again—never becoming a true disciple of Christ, because he was unwilling to sacrifice to follow the Lord.

True discipleship is rarely convenient or comfortable. In contrast to the rich young ruler, Peter and others of the Lord's disciples gave up virtually all they had in the world. The rich ruler retained his riches, but Peter, sanctified through faith and sacrifice, became endowed with a spiritual power unknown to the ruler and to all others who are unwilling to sacrifice all things for the Lord. Years later the Apostle Peter declared to the crippled man who was begging by the temple gate, "Silver and gold have I none; but such as I have give I thee: In the name of Jesus Christ of Nazareth rise up and walk" (Acts 3:6). And Peter took him by the right hand and lifted him up and he was healed. Such can be the power that accompanies a willingness to forsake all to follow Christ, for "sacrifice brings forth the blessings of heaven" (William W. Phelps, "Praise to the Man," in *Hymns,* no. 27).

Several years ago when I was teaching seminary in Arizona, we showed a Church film to the students entitled *And Should We Die.* It is a true story about Latter-day Saints from Mexico shortly after the turn of the century who were being persecuted for their religious beliefs by Zapatista rebels during the Mexican civil war. The movie focuses primarily on two LDS fathers, the branch president and his first counselor, who were imprisoned and sentenced to death. They were told that they would be spared the firing squad if they would denounce their Mormon beliefs. Because they refused to do so, the two men, President Rafael Monroy and Brother Vicente Morales, were executed in front of their families and branch members on 17 July 1915.

The students were deeply moved by the movie; many were even in tears. In this setting I asked these sobered young people, "Would you be willing to be put to death rather than denounce your faith and testimony in the restored gospel?" It was mostly a rhetorical question designed to get the students to appreciate the sacrifices made by so many for the gospel's sake. It also stimulated an examination of their own testimonies and their own commitment to the Lord. I wasn't expecting them to answer, but merely to ponder; yet some answered. At first it was only the outspoken, "macho" young men who boldy declared, "Yeah, I'd be willing to lay down my life for the Lord." Then some of the young women humbly and sweetly acknowledged that they too would "die for Jesus, because he died for me." It was a powerful moment, but the moment I shall never forget came after the bell rang, ending class. As the students were filing out of the room, one young man turned back to me and simply asked, "Brother Top, would you die for him?" He then turned and left before I could answer. I have thought of that moment many times since and have been left to wonder how I would have responded.

Perhaps my answer to the young student could have been, "Because I know that true disciples of Christ are willing to sacrifice all things, including their very lives, for the Lord and his kingdom; yes, I would do so if necessary" (see *Lectures on Faith 6:7).* Just as Adam learned that his sacrifices and burnt offerings were "a similitude of the sacrifice of the Only Begotten of the Father, which is full of grace and truth" (Moses 5:7), the complex system of sacrifices under the law of Moses was also deeply symbolic in nature. For the ancient Israelites "the whole meaning of the law, every whit [pointed] to that great and last sacrifice; and that great and last sacrifice will be the Son of God, yea, infinite and eternal" (Alma 34:14). Even today, the sacrifices required of Church members point us to Christ, reminding us of his infinite and eternal atoning sacrifice. It is one of the disciple-defining characteristics of those who sincerely seek to follow the Lord.

"I bear witness that until a person has been willing to sacrifice all he possesses in the world," President Harold B. Lee testified, "not even withholding his own life if it were necessary for the upbuilding of the kingdom, then only can he claim kinship to Him who gave his life that men might be" (in Conference Report, October 1965, p. 131). As I have pondered the deep significance of President Lee's statement and wondered within myself if I am truly willing to lay down my life and my all for the Lord, a thought seems to settle upon my mind and in my heart. It is as if I can hear the voice of the Savior saying, "I don't need you to *die* for me. I need you to *live* for me." It seems simple, yet is deeply profound. Living for the Lord, though it does not sound as dramatic, is in many ways far more demanding and a greater test of faith than dying for the Lord. It is this sentiment that is reflected in the Apostle Paul's admonition to the Roman Saints: "Present your bodies a living sacrifice" (Romans 12:1). In a similar way, the Lord condemned the Israelites who were faithful in offering the sacrifices and burnt offerings but failed in personal righteousness (see Isaiah 1:10–17). Jesus often spoke about the sacrifice that he desired of each of his disciples as a willingness to "deny himself, and take up his cross, and follow me" (Matthew 16:24).

"Submitting to the cross" is different from "taking up the cross." One describes a willingness to die for the Lord, and the other describes the kind of sacrifice that is required to live for the Lord and to faithfully follow him. "Taking up the cross" is a sacrifice that also is in similitude of the Only Begotten; not so much in that it represents his death, but rather his life—his purity and holiness. "And now for a man to take up his cross," the Savior taught, "is to deny himself all ungodliness, and every worldly lust, and keep my commandments" (JST, Matthew 16:24).

Elder Neal A. Maxwell insightfully observed: "So it is that real, personal sacrifice never was placing an animal on the altar. Instead, it is a willingness to put the animal in us upon the altar and letting it be consumed!" (In Conference Report, April 1995, p. 91.) It is this kind of sacrifice that constitutes living for the Lord. It is sacrifice that is not episodic, but continual. The Savior taught that taking up the cross is not a periodic assignment but rather a daily responsibility of discipleship. "And he said to them all, If any man will come after me, let him deny himself, and take up his cross *daily,* and follow me" (Luke 9:23; emphasis added).

What can we do to take up our cross daily? What kinds of sacrifices can we make in a down to earth, day to day, practical way that demonstrate our willingness to live for the Lord?

Keeping the Sabbath Day Holy

Am I willing to live for the Lord by keeping his holy day sacred and being willing to give up some things I like to do in order to demonstrate my faith and sacrifice? The prophet Isaiah declared the word of the Lord: "If thou turn away thy foot from the sabbath, from doing thy pleasure on my holy day; and call the sabbath a delight, the holy of the Lord, honourable; and shalt honour him, not doing thine own ways, nor finding thine own pleasure, nor speaking thine own words: Then shalt thou delight thyself in the Lord; and I will cause thee to ride upon the high places of the earth, and feed thee with the heritage of Jacob thy father: for the mouth of the Lord hath spoken it" (Isaiah 58:13–14).

The phrase "not doing thine own ways, nor finding thine own pleasure" strikes right at the heart of the issue—it illustrates that we must be willing to give up some of our own desires to do the Lord's will on his day. How could I truly lay my all on the altar of God, even sacrificing my own life if necessary, yet be unwilling to give up some of the world's ways to honor the Lord's day?

This is something that I personally have had to struggle with in my own life. I am an avid sports fan, a newsaholic, and a politics junkie. That sometimes creates a problem for me on Sundays. I want to watch news programs on television at the same time my wife wants to listen to the Tabernacle Choir broadcast. Or worse yet, I sometimes even want to watch professional football games during Sunday dinner. (Through the years I have tried to justify to my wife my watching sports on Sunday under the guise that if there were LDS players on any of the teams, I needed to "support my brethren.")

Also, for most of our married life I have been serving in a variety of leadership callings and have had to attend a lot of meetings on Sundays. Many times I would return home from the meetings and just want some quiet time and relaxation. The last thing I would want to do was play Scrabble with the family or have a family gospel discussion. It is in these kinds of dilemmas that sacrifice—living for the Lord—is most needed. I have had to ask myself the following questions:

—Am I willing to sacrifice watching games on Sunday to show the Lord that he is more important to me than sports? (Am I willing to give up watching the Super Bowl even if Steve Young is playing?)

—Am I willing to sacrifice unnecessary meetings so that I can spend more time with my family, as the Brethren intended with the implementation of the consolidated meeting schedule?

—Am I willing to sacrifice my own desires—my favorite activities or programs—to be with my family and to do things with them that will bring us closer together as a family and closer to the Lord?

—Am I willing to sacrifice my own quiet time and comfort to help my wife with dinner or to play with the children or clean up so she can have quiet time?

—Am I willing to live for the Lord by using some of the minutes of his day to study the scriptures and teach the gospel to my children? Will I sacrifice the secular for the spiritual?

Temple Attendance

Many years ago my wife and I were attending a temple session in the Arizona Temple. As we were preparing to leave, we noticed a large group of Mexican Saints enter the temple. While we were standing in the lobby watching this excited and eager group, one of the temple officiators told us that they had come by bus from Mexico, having driven for days. Many had used virtually all of their financial resources to be able to come to the temple. I was so impressed by their sacrifice.

In some parts of the world today there are those who make enormous sacrifices of time and finances to attend the temple, and yet others of us live within blocks of temples and make significantly less sacrifice to attend. When we lived in Arizona I heard Elder J. Ballard Washburn, our Regional Representative, say on several occasions, "We cannot teach our children the importance of the temple if they do not see their parents sacrificing to attend the temple often."

President Brigham Young often said that if the Saints fully understood the significance of the temple, they would be willing to walk all the way to England if necessary to participate in temple marriage (see *Journal of Discourses* 11:118). We tend to place great significance on temple marriage and the ordinances for ourselves and are willing to make great sacrifices for them. All too often, however, when we get into the mundane routine of daily life we begin to think that we are too busy with other concerns, leaving us no time to go to the temple as often as we should. Sometimes even when I go to the temple, I find myself looking at my watch often and thinking about all of the things I "should" be doing. If I am seriously seeking to be more Christlike, maybe I should sacrifice some of those "should dos" to attend the temple more often. It is within his house where I can best learn his ways. "Let us be a temple-attending people," President Howard W. Hunter urged. "Attend the temple as frequently as personal circumstances allow." (In Conference Report, October 1994, p. 8.)

I may not be required to sell my home and all my possessions to have enough money to travel great distances to attend the temple, as so many Saints in other parts of the world have done and continue to do. But how can I take up the cross of discipleship if I am unwilling to sacrifice a couple of hours to do a temple session—especially when the temple is just around the corner—or, if I have to travel greater distances to the temple, even an entire day or weekend or some of my vacation time? Am I living for the Lord when I let other, more self-centered demands on my time interfere with regular attendance at the temple? Am I showing my own family that the temple is so important to my own spiritual welfare that I am willing to give up things that I want to do or money that I could use elsewhere to participate in temple worship? How could I say that I could die for the Lord but I'm too busy or too attached to the things of the world to attend the temple?

Temple attendance almost always requires some degree of sacrifice. It is through such sacrifice that the Lord can bless us. President Gordon B. Hinckley taught:

> I urge our people everywhere, with all of the persuasiveness of which I am capable, to live worthy to hold a temple recommend, to secure one and regard it as a precious asset, and to make a greater effort to go to the house of the Lord and partake of the spirit and the blessings to be had therein. I am satisfied that every man or woman who goes to the temple in a spirit of sincerity and faith leaves the house of the Lord a better man or woman. There is need for constant improvement in all of our lives. There is need occasionally to leave the noise and the tumult of the world and step within the walls of a sacred house of God, there to feel His spirit in an environment of holiness and peace. (In Conference Report, October 1995, p. 72.)

Church Service

How could I die for the Lord if I am unwilling to take up the cross by putting my shoulder to the wheel to help push the kingdom of God along? Am I living for the Lord if I am too busy to do my home or visiting teaching? The Lord expects of us a willingness to lay not only all our earthly posssessions upon the altar for the building up of his kingdom, but also all our time, even time that is limited or inconvenient. Sacrifice of our time requires giving up some of our precious time, not just our spare time. But time is not the only sacrifice that the Savior may require of us.

When I served as a bishop and also as a counselor in the bishopric, I was sometimes dismayed when ward members would turn down callings that were extended to them. (I am not talking about those who had legitimate personal circumstances, of which we as a bishopric were unaware, that would preclude their being able to serve in that capacity.) Sometimes the response might be something like, "Oh, Bishop, I don't want to serve in the Primary. I'm too old for that. I put in my time in the Primary years ago. I would much rather be in Relief Society." Another person once declined our invitation to serve in the nursery because it was, as he said, "an under-utilization of my talents."

Perhaps there is a greater sacrifice involving more than merely our time that would be pleasing to the Lord and demonstrate our devotion to him—a sacrifice of our pride, our ego, and our personal preferences. How could I be willing to sacrifice all that I possess for the kingdom of God and yet be unwilling to serve as Scoutmaster or Primary teacher if that is what is needed of me? Maybe it is a greater sacrifice, a more faithful taking up of the cross, to truly magnify a calling that I really dislike or that brings me little personal fulfillment.

Sometimes we may unwittingly (and sometimes not so unwittingly) attach conditions to our service in the kingdom: "I'll go where you want me to go, dear Lord—as long as it's not too far. I'll do what you want me to do, dear Lord—as long as it's not too hard. I'll say what you want me to say, dear Lord—as long as it doesn't have to be to the youth." Rendering service in the Church under our own conditions is somewhat like the rich men who made their generous contributions in the temple in Jesus' day. Their contributions were not true sacrifices, because they were giving out of their abundance. Being willing to serve the Lord on his terms—even if it means that the calling is not fun or fulfilling, is not within our comfort zone of talent or preference, or is distasteful or difficult— is like the widow who cast into the treasury just two mites. "This poor widow hath cast more in, than all they which have cast into the treasury," observed Jesus. "For all they did cast in of their abundance; but she of her want did cast in all that she had, even all her living." (Mark 12:43–44.)

President Spencer W. Kimball spoke of the sacrifice of service: "We must lay on the altar and sacrifice whatever is required by the Lord. We begin by offering a 'broken heart and a contrite spirit.' We follow this by giving our best effort in our assigned fields of labor and callings. We learn our duty and execute it fully. Finally we consecrate our time, talents, and means as called upon by our . . . leaders and as prompted by the whisperings of the Spirit." (In Conference Report, April 1978, pp. 123–24.)

Home and Family

I have often teased my wife through the years that she would lie down in the road and let a dump truck run over her if it would benefit her children. (Usually when I am teasing about the way she sacrifices for her children, I am feeling sorry for myself that she doesn't show me that much attention.) It is not uncommon to hear of parents who make extraordinary sacrifices to physically protect their children, rescue them from harm, or help them succeed in life. Family life is, in and of itself, sacrifice. It is not just unselfishness and helping one another in the family that I desire to address. Another chapter will deal with Christlike love, kindness, and service in the home. Living for the Lord—taking up the cross daily—requires sacrificing those things that prevent us and our families from coming unto Christ more fully. It is the sacrificing of "little things" that will yield significant spiritual dividends of greater faith and righteousness and increased love and harmony in the home.

—Am I willing to live for the Lord by sacrificing Monday Night Football so that I can hold meaningful family home evenings with my wife and children—not just squeezing in lessons at halftime? Am I willing to sacrifice a few family night activities to balance fun with teaching the gospel to my family?

—Am I willing to sacrifice a little extra sleep or being a few minutes early to the office to gather my family together for family prayer and scripture reading?

—Am I willing to sacrifice reading the newspaper or watching the news or my favorite television program to really listen to my children and to talk with them about what they want to talk about?

—Am I willing to give up some of my time in my profession, church work, or other outside-the-home interests and activities to go to my children's activities, thereby showing them that they are more important to me than these other things?
—Am I willing to live for the Lord by sacrificing a few months of being with the grandchildren to serve a full-time mission, thus testifying to the grandchildren that my devotion to the Lord and his kingdom is paramount?
—Am I willing to sacrifice some of my personal recreation activities for family recreation?

One of our favorite family activities is to buy some treats, pop up a batch of popcorn, make some punch, and then spend a snowy day or weekend evening having a "Top Family Film Festival." Several years ago when our children were little, we had had one of these video parties and had watched three or four family films. It was quite late, and so I told the kids that they needed to go to bed.

"Why do we have to go to bed now?" my son, Justin, asked. "There's still one more video to watch." I had rented a video for Wendy and me to watch together. It was not a bad film, but was of a more mature theme. I didn't think it would be wise to let the children watch it.

"You guys can't watch this one. It's for Mom and Dad," I reasoned.

Justin's response was most profound for a young boy. "Well, if it is not good for us to watch, why can you watch it?"

Now, don't get me wrong—I recognize that sometimes there is a need for entertainment and activities on a higher intellectual level than Sesame Street or Barney the loveable purple dinosaur. I have watched *Sleeping Beauty* so many times that I can recite the dialogue backwards. I also understand that some things my kids just love cause my brain to turn into jelly, and they may feel the same about my favorite movies, music, or television programs. That's not the real issue here. Justin's words made me really stop and think what message I was giving to him. I could have tried to explain to him the whole matter and all its different implications, but no matter what I said, it still appeared that there was a double standard—that goodness, morality, and right and wrong meant something different to Mom and Dad. I had to ask myself, *Am I willing to sacrifice movies or entertainment that I wouldn't want my children to watch?* I have come to realize that no movie is so good as to be worth leaving the wrong impression in the minds of my children. Maybe Justin had it right—maybe his idea really speaks to what is most important. If it's not good for my kids, what makes it good for me? Am I willing to sacrifice any appearance of evil or double standard as I seek to teach and lead my family to seek after those things that are "virtuous, lovely, or of good report or praiseworthy"? (Articles of Faith 1:13.)

I am the light and the life of the world. I am Alpha and Omega,
the beginning and the end. . . .
And ye shall offer for a sacrifice unto me
a broken heart and a contrite spirit.
—3 Nephi 9:18, 20

Perhaps the greatest sacrifice that is needed from us as we follow Christ is to lay upon the altar of God the offering of "a broken heart and a contrite spirit" (3 Nephi 9:20). It is a life of continual repentance—of striving to live for the Lord each day by being a little more like him. Having a broken heart and a contrite spirit means having an attitude of humility and seeking to sacrifice those things that would prevent us from becoming more like the Perfect Exemplar. It involves taking up the cross and denying oneself of all ungodliness. King Lamoni's father perhaps described this kind of sacrifice best when he declared, "I will give away all my sins to know thee" (Alma 22:18). Living the law of sacrifice today may not involve persecution, expulsion from homes, or burying loved ones on the plains, as it did for our pioneer forebears. However, it does require the same level of commitment and willingness on our part to sacrifice anything that stands in the way of total commitment to the cause of Christ. "I cannot conceive of any man being able to attain unto celestial glory," Elder George Q. Cannon testified, "who is not willing to sacrifice everything that he has for the cause of God."

> Do you understand, do you comprehend, that everything we have is required by God our Father, to be laid upon the altar? Is there anything that is nearer your heart than the Gospel of the Lord Jesus Christ? Is there anything that stands between you and obedience, perfect obedience, to the will of God, as revealed unto you through the Holy Priesthood? If there is, you must get rid of it. We must humble ourselves before the Lord to that extent that we shall have a greater love of his work, a greater degree of obedience in our hearts to the Holy Priesthood than we now have for the things we so highly value. In no other way can we expect to become the people that God designs we shall be. (In *Journal of Discourses* 16:116–17.)

Now, many years after my seminary student asked me, "Brother Top, would you die for him?" I think I know the answer. My answer would have to be: "Only if I am living for him." My willingness to live for the Lord by taking up the cross daily through continual sacrifice and repentance will determine whether or not I could really die for him, for "out of small things proceedeth that which is great" (D&C 64:33).

And now, my beloved brethren, I would that ye should
come unto Christ, who is the Holy One of Israel . . .
Yea, come unto him, and offer your whole souls
as an offering unto him.
—Omni 1:26

4

Let not thy tongue give utterance to
the evil that is in thine heart, but
command thy tongue to be silent until
good shall prevail over the evil.
—President Brigham Young

Taming the Tongue

Being More Christlike in Conversation

Many years ago when my children were small, my wife prevailed upon me to "be a good father" and buy a swing-set for the family. She envisioned the children swinging and playing happily in a yard full of neighbor kids, and then she could be a "Kool-Aid Mom" by providing treats. In contrast to her vision of all the great things a swing-set would do for our children, I envisioned fights, broken arms, and worn spots on my grass.

This perception was positive, though, when compared with the very real nightmare I had when I unloaded the crate, opened the box, spread out all the pieces, and saw the plastic bag of nuts and bolts and screws. I had never seen so many pieces. I was immediately struck with horror, feeling that it would be easier to put together a five-thousand-piece jigsaw puzzle. I am a mechanical klutz—anything more mechanical than a knife and fork I can't figure out. It was quite an experience—or, more accurately stated, ordeal—for all of us to have me put together this "super-deluxe Jungle Gym" swing-set. I must admit that while I worked on this project I often thought how spoiled kids are today, and wondered, *Why can't they just occupy themselves with an empty cardboard box?*

After several days (I spent the first few days just trying to read the directions and figure out where everything was supposed to go) I was nearing the end of this monumental undertaking. Just when I was feeling pretty proud of myself and somewhat smug in my newly acquired skills, because my kids and even the neighbors recognized it as a swing-set, I encountered some difficulty getting some of the last nuts and bolts tightened down. The longer I worked at it with no success, the more frustrated I became. I huffed and puffed and muttered under my breath. All of my kids were sitting on the lawn, anxiously awaiting the completion of their new amusement park. I became exasperated with my inability to secure the final bolt, and displayed my disgust by throwing down the wrench and shouting out a slang euphemism that is common in modern vernacular. It was not one from the list of "official" swear words, mind you, but rather a commonly used replacement.

Somewhat frightened by my outburst, my daughter Jessica, who was about three years old, said quietly, "Daddy, Jesus doesn't like it when you use garbage words." Just a few weeks earlier we had had a family home evening lesson about language, and the lesson manual referred to "garbage words." I didn't think my little children even understood a thing Wendy and I had tried to teach them that night, but now I was being taught by Jessica.

In the years since, I have pondered many times Jessica's innocent yet poignant reminder to me: "Jesus doesn't like it when you use garbage words." There are so many forms of communication today that could be aptly described as garbage words, and not all of them fall into the tight little category we call profanity. The Apostle Paul used a more sophisticated term for garbage words, but the principle remains the same: "Let no *corrupt communication* proceed out of your mouth," he admonished the Ephesian Saints, "but that which is good to the use of edifying, that it may minister grace unto the hearers" (Ephesians 4:29; emphasis added).

If we are to become more Christlike, we must seek to pattern not only our actions after the Savior, but also our speech. The Apostle James taught that a person who can control his tongue is "a perfect man, and able also to bridle the whole body" (James 3:2). Taming the tongue may actually be harder than bridling behavior. It may seem like such a little thing, but the self-control required to obtain Christlike communication affects the entire soul and being of an earnest disciple.

> Behold, we put bits in the horses' mouths, that they may obey us; and we turn about their whole body.
>
> Behold also the ships, which though they be so great, and are driven of fierce winds, yet are they turned about with a very small helm, whithersoever the governor listeth.
>
> Even so the tongue is a little member, and boasteth great things. Behold, how great a matter a little fire kindleth!
>
> And the tongue is a fire, a world of iniquity: so is the tongue among our members, that it defileth the whole body, and setteth on fire the course of nature; and it is set on fire of hell.
>
> For every kind of beasts, and of birds, and of serpents, and of things in the sea, is tamed, and hath been tamed of mankind:
>
> But the tongue can no man tame; it is an unruly evil, full of deadly poison.
>
> Therewith bless we God, even the Father; and therewith curse we men, which are made after the similitude of God.
>
> Out of the same mouth proceedeth blessing and cursing. My brethren, these things ought not so to be. (James 3:3–10.)

"Garbage words" or "corrupt communication" comes in a wide array of faces, some more obvious than others; yet all are poisonous to the soul and barriers to becoming more like the Savior. As we seek to emulate the Great Exemplar, we must, spiritually speaking, "wash our mouths out" with the soap of repentance and self-control. By eliminating the forms of corrupt communication I will discuss here, we can become examples "of the believers, in word [and] in conversation" (1 Timothy 4:12).

PROFANITY

One of my students came to me one day seeking advice as to how she could get some of her friends to stop swearing. My immediate reaction was, "Just ask them to stop. Tell them that it is offensive to you and if they care at all about you they would stop. And besides, they are members of the Church and they should know that what you are saying is right." She told me that she had already tried that, and the response from one of the returned-missionary friends totally left her not knowing how to respond. "Come on," he had said, "swearing isn't that terrible of a sin. Haven't you ever heard of J. Golden Kimball? He was a General Authority and even swore in general conference."

How could she respond to that? A General Authority who swears in conference (and the continuing J. Golden stories that bring chuckles to the Saints) almost appears to validate that profanity, "as long as it's not too bad," is no big deal. I thought about how I could help my student be able to respond adequately to this prevailing attitude. Then it dawned on me that it doesn't matter if J. Golden Kimball swore, or any other General Authority, or our favorite bishop, or even a BYU religion professor. It is not them that we seek to emulate. It is the Savior after whom we pattern our lives, and he has commanded us "for the works which ye have seen me do that shall ye also do" (3 Nephi 27:21).

The word *profanity* comes from the root *profane,* which has direct reference to blaspheming the name of Deity. I find it interesting yet troubling that although there are swear words not allowed on television, the sacred names of God are repeatedly used in all manner of irreverent exclamations. Taking the name of God in vain, which Jehovah declared to Moses from Sinai was to be punished by death, is not even considered by many in our society to be an expletive. Such profaning of the name of God reflects a lack of respect, love, and appreciation for what our Heavenly Father and his Only Begotten Son have done for us. It is an offensive affront to the Supreme Being to whom we are indebted for all we have and are, and to all who recognize that indebtedness.

President Spencer W. Kimball illustrated this principle with an experience he had in his own life: "In the hospital one day I was wheeled out of the operating room by an attendant who stumbled, and there issued from his angry lips vicious cursing with a combination of the names of the Savior. Even half-conscious, I recoiled and implored: "Please! Please! That is my Lord whose names you revile." There was a deathly silence, then a subdued voice whispered: "I am sorry." (*The Teachings of Spencer W. Kimball,* ed. Edward L. Kimball [Salt Lake City: Bookcraft, 1982], p. 198.)

No person who is seriously seeking to be more Christlike would ever think that taking the name of God in vain is in any way acceptable before the Lord. How can anyone who loves the Lord, has felt his love in his own life, and has a sense of gratitude for his relationship to God defile and irreverence, either in anger or flippancy, the sacred names of Deity? It is the antithesis of speaking with the "tongue of angels" (2 Nephi 31:13). It is the blasphemous discourse of devils. "Do angels take the Lord's name in vain?" asked President George Q. Cannon.

> The idea is so ridiculous that we scarcely like to ask the question. . . . How dare we do that which angels dare not do? Is is possible for us to argue that that which is forbidden in heaven is praiseworthy on earth? . . .
>
> Though we are sure no boy can tell us any advantage that can arise from the abuse of God's holy name, yet we can tell him many evils that arise therefrom. To begin, it is unnecessary and consequently foolish; it lessens our respect for holy things and leads us into the society of the wicked; it brings upon us the disrespect of the good who avoid us; it leads us to other sins, for he who is willing to abuse his Creator is not ashamed to defraud his fellow creature; and also by so doing we directly and knowingly break one of the most direct of God's commandments. (In *Juvenile Instructor,* 27 September 1873, p. 156.)

Profanity has become broader than merely profaning God's name. While most Latter-day Saints decry the use of God's name and would seek never to do so themselves, there are many who are not as firm in their view of other forms of swearing. Sometimes it is even viewed as cute, macho, or the sophisticated thing to do.

While our family was sitting at the breakfast table many years ago, we had an experience that illustrated to us how swearing can creep almost innocently, yet insidiously, into our everyday vocabulary. I was putting mustard on my scrambled eggs, when Tiffany, our three-year-old daughter, said matter-of-factly, "What in the ——— are you putting on your eggs?" The other children burst out laughing, and Wendy and I gasped in horror and in unison cried out, "Tiffany!"

Realizing that we were shocked and unhappy with her statement, she burst into tears. We comforted her and told her that we were not mad at her, but merely stunned that such a word would come out of the mouth of our three-year-old. We asked her where she had heard the word, and she responded that she had heard it many times on television and from the kids in the neighborhood and as a result didn't think there was anything wrong with it. Needless to say, we had an important teaching moment while we finished our breakfast.

It is one thing for a three-year-old, who doesn't know any better to use swear words to "spice up" her vocabulary, but it is totally unbecoming of all who seek to be more like the Master both in word and deed. Someone once insightfully observed, "Profanity is the attempt of a feeble mind to express itself forcibly." When one uses profanity, either in anger or in jest, it reflects the corrupt communication of a natural man rather than the communication of one whose thoughts and words are garnished with virtue unceasingly (see D&C 121:45). President Kimball observed: "We note the increasing coarseness of language and understand how Lot must have felt when he was, according to Peter, 'vexed with the filthy conversation of the wicked' (2 Peter 2:7). We wonder why those of coarse and profane conversation, even if they refuse obedience to God's will, are so stunted mentally that they let their capacity to communicate grow more and more narrow. Language is like music; we rejoice in beauty, range, and quality in both, and we are demeaned by the repetition of a few sour notes." (*The Teachings of Spencer W. Kimball*, p. 199.)

President Kimball used the phrase "coarseness of language." This phrase, I believe, includes more than profaning the name of God and swearing. It also includes filthy and foul talk such as slang euphemisms, dirty jokes, "bathroom talk," and sexual innuendoes. In some ways this type of corrupt communication is more debased and demeaning than profanity alone. It grieves the Spirit of the Lord and may indicate what is not only in the minds of the users but also in their hearts. How can such talk, if not checked by repentance, help but lead to filthy and vulgar behavior? As Elder Neal A. Mawell observed: "Why should we expect those who 'mind the things of the flesh' to mind their tongues? (Romans 8:5.)" (In Conference Report, April 1995, p. 89.)

A few years ago I went to a local fast-food restaurant near the BYU campus for lunch. I arrived about the same time that Provo High School was dismissing for its lunch hour, and soon all of the booths were filled with chattering high school students. I found myself sitting in a booth adjacent to a group of Provo High girls. They looked like typical LDS young women, which is a pretty good assumption, considering the overwhelming number of Latter-day Saints in Utah County. I soon became shocked, then disgusted, and ultimately sickened by their foul talk. They were not swearing or blaspheming God's name, but their conversation was filled with filthy slang words and flippant discussions of immoral behaviors. I am not prudish, nor have I lived a totally sheltered life, but I must admit I was disgusted by their talk that "would have made a truck driver blush." Perhaps many, if not most or all of them, faithfully kept the Word of Wisdom and would never consider letting a cigarette or beer touch their lips; yet they did not realize that as Jesus declared, "Not that which goeth into the mouth defileth a man; but that which cometh out of the mouth, this defileth a man. Do not ye yet understand, that whatsoever entereth in at the mouth goeth into the belly, and is cast out into the draught? But those things which proceed out of the mouth come forth from the heart; and they defile the man. For out of the heart proceed evil thoughts, murders, adulteries, fornications, thefts, false witness, blasphemies: These are the things which defile a man." (Matthew 15:11, 17–20.)

There have been times when we have been watching a television program or a video as a family, and my wife will say something to the effect of, "Do we have to listen to this?" The children will sometimes say, "Oh, Mom, it's not that bad. They are not even swearing. We hear a lot worse than this at school." It doesn't matter if the "official" swear words are being used or if there is explicit sexual talk. It is corrupt communication when coarse, crude, and offensive speech is uttered, whether slang or innuendo; and we who seek to pattern our lives after the Savior should avoid such. "Stay out of the gutter in your conversation," President Gordon B. Hinckley exhorted the Saints in a general priesthood meeting. "Foul talk defiles the man [or woman] who speaks it."

> Can you think of a missionary in this church using the kind of language heard on many high school campuses? Of course not. Such would be totally out of character with his calling as an ambassador of the Lord.
>
> . . . It is as wrong for you to use foul language as it would be for a missionary. . . . Remember that it is the same voice which prays to the Lord on the one hand and which, on the other hand, when in the company of friends, may be inclined so to speak language foul and filthy. The two kinds of voices are incompatible.
>
> Paul, perhaps the greatest missionary of all time, wrote to Timothy, his young associate in the ministry. "Let no man despise thy youth," he said, "but be thou an example of the believers, in word, in conversation, in charity, in spirit, in faith, in purity" (1 Timothy 4:12).
>
> Note what he says: "Be thou an example *in word.*" He is speaking here of language. I think he is speaking of the things of which I have been speaking. He is saying that coarse and lewd words are incompatible with one's calling as a believer in Christ.
>
> "In conversation"—he is saying again that in our dialogues with others we must be an example of the believer. Conversation is the substance of friendly social activity. It can be happy. It can be light. It can be earnest. It can be funny. But it must not be salty, or uncouth, or foul if one is in sincerity a believer in Christ.
>
> . . . It is a tragic and unnecessary thing that boys and girls use foul language. It is inexcusable for a girl so to speak. It is likewise serious for the boy who holds the priesthood. This practice is totally unacceptable for one authorized to speak in the name of God. To blaspheme His holy name or to speak in language that is debached is offensive to God and man.
>
> The man or the boy [or woman or girl] who must resort to such language immediately says that he is poverty-ridden in his vocabulary. He [or she] does not enjoy sufficient richness of expression to be able to speak effectively without swearing or using foul words. . . .
>
> I say this to the boys [and girls]. I say it also to any of you older men [and women] who have a similar problem. I do so with love. I

know that the Lord is pleased when we use clean and virtuous language, for He has set an example for us. His revelations are couched in words that are affirmative, that are uplifting, that encourage us to do what is right and to go forward in truth and goodness.

Don't swear. Don't profane. Avoid so-called dirty jokes. Stay away from conversation that is sprinkled with foul and filthy words. You will be happier if you do so, and your example will give strength to others. (In Conference Report, October 1987, pp. 57, 58, 59.)

Speaking Lightly of Sacred Things

In ancient times, Jehovah's commandment to Moses and his people, "Thou shalt not take the name of the Lord thy God in vain," meant much more than we usually attribute to that command today. It included not only blaspheming the name of God but also making a covenant in the name of God and then breaking that covenant, speaking of or taking oaths in the name of pagan gods, and speaking of God and sacred things in any irreverent, sacrilegious, or contemptuous manner. So serious was such defiled discourse that death was the punishment. (See Exodus 22:28; 23:13; Leviticus 19:12; 24:10–16.)

Today, profaning the name of God means more than just swearing or cursing. The word *profane* literally means "showing contempt or irreverence toward God or sacred things; to put to an improper, unworthy, or degrading use." Unfortunately, there are those who would never let the name of God spew from their lips in a cursing or blasphemous manner yet who profane his name in other more common but less apparent ways. "Behold, I am Alpha and Omega, even Jesus Christ," the Lord proclaimed to the Saints of this dispensation. "Wherefore, let all men beware how they take my name in their lips." (D&C 63:60–61.)

Corrupt communication could include any language, whether swearing or not, that makes sacred things common and lacks proper reverence, even awe, for God and his ways. This is done all too frequently in many homes and wards today, almost unthinkingly. For example, we would never come home from the temple, having made sacred covenants not to divulge things that transpire there, and then flippantly use temple language or even speak openly of those sacred covenants and ordinances. Yet often we speak flippantly, even carnally, of the body, which is a temple of God; and of the powers of procreation, which are in very deed the sacred powers of godliness. Sometimes we joke about, speak euphemistically, and make common that which is both physically and spiritually most intimate. Bishop H. Burke Peterson declared, "Some demonstrate or express a personal weakness when they tell jokes or stories about the body and its functions, when they joke about or make suggestive comments concerning women or girls, when they are casual about sacred things. . . . Some married couples will even joke about sexual matters. Each of these kinds of experiences will weaken any spirit and will make it less able to withstand the fiery darts of the adversary." ("Purify Your Thoughts," in *Brigham Young University 1983–84 Fireside and Devotional Speeches* [Provo, Utah: University Publications, 1984], p. 20.) Such talk is corrupt in that it is after the manner of the natural or corruptible man, not that of the divine or incorruptible. As it says in the Doctrine and Covenants 63:64, "Remember that that which cometh from above is sacred, and must be spoken with care, and by constraint of the Spirit." In section 6 we read, "Trifle not with sacred things" (verse 12).

Another way that we may profane sacred things, or make them common or treat them with irreverence, is by talking too frequently, openly, or casually about spiritual experiences and personal promptings of the Spirit. We must speak of those kinds of impressions only as the Spirit directs and only with deep reverence and gratitude, never wearing spirituality on our sleeves either by word or attitude. "I have learned that strong, impressive spiritual experiences do not come to us very frequently," Elder Boyd K. Packer taught. "And when they do, they are generally for our own edification, instruction, or correction. . . . I have come to believe also that it is not wise to continually talk of unusual spiritual experiences. They are to be guarded with care and shared only when the Spirit itself prompts us to use them to the blessing of others." (*That All May Be Edified* [Salt Lake City: Bookcraft, 1982], p. 337.)

Lying

"These six things doth the Lord hate," the ancient Israelite proverb attributed to King Solomon states, "yea, seven are an abomination unto him: a proud look, *a lying tongue,* and hands that shed innocent blood, an heart that deviseth wicked imaginations, feet that be swift in running to mischief, *a false witness that speaketh lies,* and he that soweth discord among brethren" (Proverbs 6:16–19; emphasis added). Interestingly, lying is mentioned twice among the seven sins hated by the Lord. In our own day, the Lord graphically portrayed the spiritual seriousness of lying when he declared that "all liars, and whosoever loveth and maketh a lie, . . . shall have their part in that lake which burneth with fire and brimstone, which is the second death" (D&C 63:17; see also D&C 76:103–6).

No one can doubt the seriousness of lying, as taught in the scriptures both ancient and modern and by the words of living prophets. I don't think the temptation to make bold, bald-faced lies is a major stumbling block to a serious disciple of Christ. Such a person clearly seeks to avoid the "big lies." While these blatant and overt lies may be compared to giant boulders blocking the strait and narrow path, "little white lies" are like pebbles or gravel that cause us to spin our wheels in the pathway of discipleship. Becoming more Christlike requires the elimination from our lives of the seemingly harmless little white lies as well as the "big whoppers" that are designed to deceive and hurt.

One of my favorite Disney movies is *Pinocchio.* As a child I laughed with delight when Pinocchio would fib and his nose would grow. Now, as an adult, I find myself looking at the story in a slightly different light. Instead of fantasy and entertainment alone, I see an important lesson about honesty that needs remembering. I have since thought that maybe it would not be all bad if our noses were to suddenly grow each time we lied, the length of growth in proportion to the "size" and seriousness of the lie. Our lying, whether simple or serious, would be readily apparent to all. It wouldn't take long for us to realize that little white lies have an adverse effect upon us, just like "big, bad, black lies." I wouldn't have to wait until I sprouted donkey ears to realize that maybe I just shouldn't lie at all. My nose is already long enough.

President Howard W. Hunter admonished the Saints to think more often of the Savior and to ask themselves, "What would Jesus do?" In applying this counsel to my own life, I have tried to imagine Jesus saying some of the things that have come from my own mouth and from the lips of so many others who profess to be his disciples. For example, I can't imagine the Savior saying to family or friends, "Tell them I'm not here!" when there is a knock on the door. Nor can I fathom him fudging just a little in his dealings with others. Somehow it seems totally incongruous with his divine nature to even tell little white lies, no matter how justifiable they may seem.

I am reminded of this concept quite often when my wife asks me some of life's toughest questions such as "How do I look?" or "Did you like that new recipe I tried tonight?" or "You're not angry with me for denting the car, are you?" (Perhaps every husband has faced such moments of truth and has wrestled with the seeming conflict between total honesty and needed sensitivity.) Sometimes we may feel that lying may be all right if there is a noble objective or higher purpose to be attained by such dishonesty. I know I have been guilty of that—like the night my home teachers showed up without an appointment right at the most exciting part of a triple-overtime BYU basketball game. "We didn't catch you at a bad time, did we?" "Oh, no," I responded, "we're glad you came over." I was lying through my teeth, but I felt that it seemed rather selfish to say a home teaching visit should take a backseat to a sporting event.

I have had numerous experiences where a little white lie seemed appropriate or helpful at the time, but now I must ask myself, "How would Jesus respond?" Sometimes he was brutally honest, such as when he condemned the hyprocritical scribes and pharisees. At other times he didn't say everything he knew or could have said, and at times he responded with silence. But never do we see him lying. "Just tell the truth" remains the best advice for all. Sometimes the truth must be tempered with other Christlike attributes such as kindness, love, and mercy. Perhaps the key to Christlike communication is to be totally honest and perfectly kind at the same time, or, as Elder Neal A. Maxwell said, to speak with "candor in the context of love" (*"A More Excellent Way"* [Salt Lake City: Deseret Book Co., 1967], p. 118).

The scriptures describe Satan as "a liar from the beginning" (D&C 93:25) and as "the father of all lies" (2 Nephi 2:18) who "flattereth [people], and telleth them that it is no sin to lie" (D&C 10:25). In contrast, Jesus is the antithesis of Lucifer—he is all that Satan isn't, and is the very personification of truth (see John 14:6). In this context, we can see lying as the essence of Lucifer himself. There can be no such thing then as just a harmless little white lie any more than there can be just a little harmless bit of Lucifer in us. If I am truly seeking to be more like Jesus in my life, I must rid myself not only of the "big boulder lies," but also the "gravel lies." The elimination of the corrupt communication of lying requires that I search my soul in each situation and ensure that my communication, like the Savior's, is devoid of deception or evasion. "Do not let us lie at all," John Ruskin admonished. "Do not think of one falsity as harmless, and another as slight, and another as unintended. Cast them all aside; they may be light and accidental, but . . . it is better that our hearts should be swept clean of them." (As cited in *Richard Evans' Quote Book* [Salt Lake City: Publishers Press, 1971], p. 186.)

Gossip

The Greek word from which *corrupt* in the phrase *corrupt communication* comes implies not only something evil but also something harmful, hurtful, or malicious. Few other forms of corrupt communication can be more harmful and hurtful than gossip. Proverbs 18:8 speaks of the hurtful nature of this kind of "corrupt communication" when it declares, "The words of a talebearer are as wounds, and they go down into the innermost parts of the belly." Hopefully none of us would ever openly and consciously inflict physical pain and suffering upon someone; yet gossip, even if not maliciously intended, not only inflicts emotional and spiritual pain upon the target of the gossip but also can lead to reputations being ruined and lives left in shambles. It may seem such an innocuous thing, but it can lead to disaster. Elder Gene R. Cook illustrates the seriousness of gossip with the following true story:

> Solemnly, people began to gather outside the mission president's office. Exchanging astonished glances, many could still not believe that they had been summoned to a church court. The officers of the court were full of love and understanding, but very serious in their investigation of the charges; those present could lose their membership in The Church of Jesus Christ of Latter-day Saints. The charge was not immorality or apostasy; they were accused of speaking evil of a neighbor.
>
> A fine brother had been slandered by those gathered together that evening, accused of the serious charge of immorality. He was completely innocent, but the great damage that had been done by "those whom he counted as his friends" would not be easily repaired. Who could measure the near destruction of this good soul? Who could measure the impact on the branch, as its fellowship was eroded? And what about the effect on those nonmembers who also became involved? Who could ever undo the evil that had affected hundreds of lives?
>
> It happened so easily. It began with simple words like—
>
> "Did you hear. . . ?"
>
> "Sister Joan said. . . ."
>
> "I have heard that he told her. . . ."
>
> "I am not sure about this, but. . . ."
>
> "Mr. Sanchez's cousin said that he thought. . . ."
>
> "I don't want to say anything bad, but. . . ."
>
> "If you won't repeat this, I guess I could tell you that. . . ."
>
> Sin has many tools, the saying goes, but a lie is the handle that fits them all. If you are one of those who think it permissible to tell white lies, you may soon find yourself color-blind. . . .
>
> Some may think they build their self-esteem and gain the attention and respect of others by bearing false tales, but they actually become Satan's agents. ("Gossip," *Ensign*, January 1981, p. 27.)

I have seen in our own family how we sometimes minimize the seriousness of talking behind others' backs. While we readily recognize that lying and bearing false witness about someone is wrong, the line between being a malicious talebearer and engaging in idle gossip often becomes somewhat blurred. There have been many times when my wife and I overheard our children talking disparagingly about someone. My wife would speak up and say something like, "Don't be a gossip!" And often their response was something to the effect of, "Oh, Mom, we are not gossiping. Everything we are saying is true." They didn't seem to realize that just because what they were saying was true, it was still gossip—hurtful and unbecoming of one who seeks to emulate the Master. Whether such corrupt communication overtly harms another, it certainly harms the one who speaks it. "A man cannot speak but he judges himself," wrote Ralph Waldo Emerson. "With his will, or against his will, he draws his portrait to the eye of his companions by every word. Every opinion reacts on him who utters it." (As cited in *Richard Evans' Quote Book,* p. 189.) Words of gossip, whatever the motivation, "are as wounds, and they go down into the innermost parts of the belly" of the person who speaks them (Proverbs 18:8). President Joseph F. Smith taught: "To be thus engaged [in gossip] is a positive injury, also, to the person so employed, because, by constantly holding the defects of others in his own mind, he ruins his own ability to see and appreciate the virtues of his fellows, thus stifling his nobler self. It is so very much better for a person to strive to develop himself by observing all the good points he can find in others, than to strangle the growth of his better self by cherishing a fault-finding, sullen, and intermeddling spirit." (*Gospel Doctrine* [Salt Lake City: Deseret Book Co., 1939], p. 112.)

In our home we have often used the old adage "If you can't say anything nice, don't say anything at all." But as we seek to become more Christlike it is apparent that silence, or the mere avoidance of gossip and speaking evil of one another, is not enough in our quest to emulate the Savior. To us today, the Lord has issued both do's and don'ts with regard to our communication with and about others:

—"Therefore, strengthen your brethren in all your conversation, in all your prayers, in all your exhortations, and in all your doings" (D&C 108:7).

—"Cease to contend one with another; cease to speak evil one of another. . . . And let your words tend to edifying one another" (D&C 136:23–24).

Criticism, Negativism, and Contention

While serving my mission in Denmark, my companion and I had an experience that taught us the adverse effects that result from continual negativism, criticism, and backbiting. Because our success in teaching people had been quite limited, it became easy to fall into a rut of discouragement. Discouragement and its twin sister, negativism, weaken the spirit and open the door to other vices. We found that in this weakened condition it became difficult for us to see anything in a positive light. After each rejection we found ourselves making critical comments about the person. The more doors that were slammed in our faces, the more critical and negative we became. Soon the criticism broadened to include the person's dog, yard, flowers, and even the color of their house. In retrospect I can see how silly we were acting, but at the time we felt justified in our critical outlook on everything, because, we thought, it was really their fault for not accepting the gospel. We soon recognized that this attitude not only was affecting us on the inside but probably was apparent on the outside. It was almost as if we, like cartoon characters, were walking around with dark storm clouds hovering over our heads. We were actually wearing our badges of negativism on our sleeves, and no one wanted to have anything to do with us, lest the storm clouds "rain on their parade."

It was at the darkest moment of discouragement that I remembered something our mission president had shared with us. He told of an experience that he had had as a missionary in Denmark many years earlier with Elder Spencer W. Kimball, who was touring the mission. With every comment the mission president said that was of a negative or critical cast, Elder Kimball would respond with something positive. The mission president and his young assistant (who was to become my mission president) hadn't realized this until one day when they drove by an unkempt woman in tattered clothes, with several children following behind. The children had dirty faces and ragged clothes.

"Look at that," the mission president observed. "Isn't that just awful? That mother should take better care of those children so they don't look so dirty and uncared for."

"Yes," Elder Kimball stated, "but aren't they beautiful?" With that simple response, all recognized that you can either spend your time looking at the negative, or seeing the glass as half empty; or you can accentuate the positive, or see the glass as half full.

Our mission president had told us that story to remind us of the need to have a positive attitude and to look for the good in all people, situations, and circumstances. My companion and I set a goal to refrain from being critical and negative in any way for at least one week. Our goal was severely tested with the first door slammed in our faces, but we bit our lips and tried to say something positive—even though it was feigned at the time. It wasn't very long until we experienced a miracle. We were soon being invited into homes to share our testimonies, rather than having doors slammed in our faces. Discouragement was displaced by enthusiasm. Criticism was replaced with compassion and praise. Negativism was swallowed up by hope for a brighter day and gratitude for blessings. When our critical thoughts and words ceased, we rose above the storm clouds of negativism and cynicism and discovered that, spiritually speaking, the air was cleaner and the view was clearer than we had experienced while down in the dumps.

From this experience, and many others since, I have learned that being critical, cynical, and negative often harms ourselves more than others. Backbiting and contention retard the Spirit of the Lord in our lives, and as a result our worship of the Lord and service in His kingdom is hampered. So fundamental is this principle that even in sacred places we are taught that the Spirit of the Lord is withdrawn when hearts are filled with unkind feelings and lips utter criticism and contention. At the organization of his church in these latter days, the Lord admonished the Saints that there should not be any "hardness with each other, neither lying, backbiting, nor evil speaking" (D&C 20:54).

Not long ago I watched an interesting program on television about acupuncture. I can't really remember very much about the program or the suggested benefits of the procedure, because I was so taken aback by the images of twenty or thirty needles being stuck into various parts of the patient's body. Maybe I'm just a wimp and "needle-phobic," but that image stuck with me (no pun intended) and I have thought how words can often be like needle pricks—sometimes only inflicting brief discomfort, and at other times inflicting deeper and more lasting pain.

We have a lot of fun in our family and experience our full share of laughter. Some of this joking is in the form of teasing or sarcasm. This is mostly good-natured and loving, but sometimes it crosses over the line and becomes hurtful. My teenage children have taught me to be more careful with my words. Sometimes when I am teasing one of the children, the others might say "Ouch!" at my comment, which is their way of saying that my sarcasm or teasing had a bite or "needle prick" to it that, though unintended, could hurt feelings. Even the children themselves will sometimes say something mean and then try to minimize the pain by quickly responding, "Just kidding!" That doesn't take away the damaging effects any more than someone who stabs another with a knife and then says "Oops," thinking that exclamation will take away the pain and heal the wound. I can't imagine the Perfect Judge excusing hurtful words, belittling sarcasm, constant criticism, or contentious conflict just because the guilty person afterwards states, "Just kidding!"

Contention and criticism and "hardness with each other" may be the most malicious and damaging form of corrupt communication. King Benjamin's counsel to watch our words applies to us in all aspects of our lives (see Mosiah 4:30). The real proving ground for Christlike living, however, is within the walls of our own homes. I am not a serious disciple of Christ if I can temper my tongue with colleagues at work or members of my ward with whom I serve, but then pinprick and wound the tender feelings of my own family. Most of the time the pinpricks that are inflicted upon family members are over the most insignificant matters. "We sometimes nag the people we love the best over little inattentions, small faults, mere nothings in the whole scheme of things," Elder Paul H. Dunn observed.

> Instead of treasuring the all-too-rare moments we share with our dear ones, we pick at faults, imagined or otherwise. How many of us say to our wives, our husbands, our children: "Why can't you do this?" "Why don't you do that?" Or "Someday when I have the time . . ."
>
> Our last daughter left for college this past month, and the eighteen years of daily living with her were suddenly over. Where had they gone? What minute, what hour, what day or night had swallowed up all those joyous, giggling, growing-up years? The first night she was away, I slipped into her bedroom, looked at her record player, and thought of all those times I had mechanically said, "Would you turn down the music!" And I thought, too, how often in the days ahead we'd be longing to hear the music. . . .
>
> Why do those sudden moments of clarity, when we realize how precious our loved ones are, come so rarely? How do we let ourselves get caught up in fault-finding, digging, or scolding at those who are nearest our hearts? Is it ever worth it? As C. S. Lewis once advised, "Take care. It is so easy to break eggs without making omelettes." . . .
>
> . . . Does it have to take flights away from home, a child leaving for college, or the death of a husband who will never again leave his hat in an awkward place to remind us how sweet are the moments with our loved ones and friends? How brief they are in the run of time? Does it take these things to stop us in our picking at trifling faults to realize the beauty of every minute together? (In Conference Report, October 1977, pp. 35, 36.)

There are times when criticism may be needed, but *how* it is rendered is more important than *who* receives it and *when* it is received. "Reproving betimes with sharpness, when moved upon by the Holy Ghost; and then showing forth afterwards an increase of love toward him whom thou hast reproved, lest he esteem thee to be his enemy" (D&C 121:43). As we seek to correct with kindness rather than to criticize or contend, it would be well to remember the following observation of Elder James E. Faust: "I recently heard in a special place, 'Your criticism may be worse than the conduct you are trying to correct' " (in Conference Report, October 1987, p. 42).

A short story written by Nathaniel Hawthorne entitled "The Birthmark" profoundly illustrates the destructive nature of faultfinding. In this story a scientist named Aylmer marries a beautiful woman named Georgiana who is perfect in almost every way. However, she possesses one slight defect—a small crimson birthmark on her cheek. Prior to the marriage Aylmer had paid no attention to the birthmark, but soon after he becomes almost obsessed with this imperfection. It seems as if all he can see is the birthmark. Aylmer overlooks Georgiana's natural beauty, grace and charms, and depth of character as he focuses more and more upon what he perceives as a gross imperfection.

An alchemist by trade, Aylmer soon begins to concoct a chemical potion that will cause the birthmark to fade until finally it will disappear completely. Georgiana at first rejects the idea of being submitted to the treatment, worried that it could cause permanent damage; but she relents because she recognizes that her husband can never look beyond the crimson mark. He assures her that the chemical treatment will indeed cause the birthmark to disappear, and then she will truly be perfect in his eyes in every way.

Aylmer carefully prepares his chemical potion and presents it to Georgiana to drink, confident that soon the small birthmark that has troubled him so will be gone forever. After Georgiana drinks the potion, they sit down together to watch the defect disappear. It begins to fade, just as Aylmer has predicted. Soon it is barely visible, but to their horror, the side effects of this treatment are making Georgiana deathly ill. By the time the birthmark has completely dissolved, it is apparent that Aylmer's beloved wife is dying. As she breathes her last, Aylmer comes to the horrible realization that he has destroyed that which he holds most dear by his fatal fixation on a single fault.

Each time I read this story I think how similar criticism and faultfinding are to Aylmer's experiment. We often overlook the good and instead become fixated on faults and failings and imperfections of others. We often suppose our criticism and naggings will eliminate the perceived defects in others, when in reality we actually inflict harm rather than healing and destroy rather than strengthen.

Continual complaining, like criticism, backbiting, and contention, is also a form of corrupt communication that must be eliminated if we are to become Christlike in conversation as well as in deed. Complaining and negativism may not overtly or maliciously harm another, but they repel the Spirit within us because they reflect both a lack of faith in the Lord's promises and an ingratitude for the bounties the Lord has proffered us. We need not be Pollyanna-like or naively view everything through rose-colored glasses, but we can focus on the goodness of others and life itself rather than dwelling on the negative, both in our minds and with our words. Just as edifying words will build and strengthen others, continual complaints and negative comments wear upon the hearers as well as the speaker and weigh the spirit down.

Jesus seeks to lift us up, not drag us down. It is his perfect example that we should seek to emulate, even with our words. "I am asking that we stop seeking out the storms," President Gordon B. Hinckley admonished, "and enjoy more fully the sunlight."

> Criticism, faultfinding, evil speaking—these are of the spirit of our day. . . . Everywhere is heard the snide remark, the sarcastic gibe, the cutting down of associates. Sadly, these are too often the essence of our conversation. In our homes, wives weep and children give up under the barrage of criticism leveled by husbands and fathers. Criticism is the forerunner of divorce, the cultivator of rebellion, sometimes a catalyst that leads to failure. In the Church it sows the seed of inactivity and finally apostasy.
>
> . . . I am suggesting that as we go through life we "accentuate the positive." I am asking that we look a little deeper for the good, that we still voices of insult and sarcasm, that we more generously compliment virtue and effort. I am not asking that all criticism be silenced. Growth comes of correction. Strength comes of repentance. Wise is the man who can acknowledge mistakes pointed out by others and change his course.
>
> What I am suggesting is that each of us turn from the negativism that so permeates our society and look for the remarkable good among those with whom we associate, that we speak of one

> another's virtues more than we speak of one another's faults, that optimism replace pessimism, that our faith exceed our fears. When I was a young man and was prone to speak critically, my father would say: "Cynics do not contribute, skeptics do not create, doubters do not achieve."
>
> Looking at the dark side of things always leads to a spirit of pessimism which so often leads to defeat. ("The Continuing Pursuit of Truth," *Ensign*, April 1986, pp. 2–4.)

Just as my daughter reminded me so many years ago that "Jesus doesn't like it when we use garbage words," the Apostle Paul condemned "corrupt communication." The Greek word from which *corrupt* comes also implies something that is rotten. Garbage that isn't dumped soon becomes rotten. Similarly, spiritual garbage, if not repented of and eliminated from our lives, will also cause spiritual decay. In our quest to become more like the Savior, we must "dump the garbage words" from our conversation so that spirituality and sensitivity do not rot within us. Christlike communication, the opposite of corrupt communication, requires lips that speak no evil. We must seek not only to do what the Lord would do but also to say what he would say.

Using Words That Build

Taming the tongue not only requires eliminating garbage words and any form of corrupt communication from our lips, but also replacing it with Christlike communication—words that build rather than tear down, heal rather than hurt. "Therefore, strengthen your brethren in all your conversation," the Lord admonished us, "in all your prayers, in all your exhortations, and in all your doings" (D&C 108:7). Taming the tongue involves also training the tongue. To say what Jesus would say involves more than just avoiding things he wouldn't say. There are words and phrases that strengthen relationships, instill a positive feeling in others, and endear others to us. These godly words and strengthening conversations include such simple phrases as "I'm sorry," "Excuse me," "Thank you," and "Please forgive me."

When we lived in Israel I was amazed at the lack of common courtesy there. I don't think that this phenomenon is unique to Israel—it is all too prevalent in virtually all parts of the world today. When a group of students would arrive in Jerusalem and I would lead them on their first orientation tour of the city, I would often take them to the bus stop and say, "I want to introduce you to Israeli bus etiquette." The students would studiously observe the people, expecting to learn some new cultural gem. After a moment of observation, they would burst out laughing and recognize my "assignment" for the joke that it was. They would see people pushing and shoving, even sometimes yelling at each other. Israeli bus etiquette was in reality the survival of the fittest and fastest. I wanted the students to see the lack of common courtesy and seek to fill the void with Christlike phrases such as "Excuse me," "After you," or "You can have my seat."

There was a word in Hebrew that I tried to use frequently but hardly if ever heard someone else say: *slichah,* "excuse me." In fact, I was amused to see people's faces at the grocery store or on the bus when I accidently bumped into them or was in their way and would state in the best Hebrew I could muster, *"Slichah"*—"Excuse me." They looked at me like I was crazy. At first I wondered if I had said it right. I checked the Hebrew-English dictionary and practiced my pronunciation, and the people I spoke to still had that funny look on their faces. Then it dawned on me that it wasn't the word or my bad pronunciation. It was that, although the word does indeed exist in the Hebrew vocabulary, it is so rarely spoken that people are usually surprised by a simple word of courtesy.

I have thought many times how, right here around us, even perhaps in our own homes, there are words that actually exist in the English vocabulary but are so rarely heard that someone may be shocked by our using them. Several years ago there was a popular television series called *Happy Days.* In one of the episodes the star of the show, Fonzie, a 50s type "greaser" and tough guy, tried to say the words "I'm sorry." Every time he tried make that statement he would choke on his words and could never spit it out. It was hilarious watching him try to say something that needed to be said but was so out of character for him. He considered himself too cool to apologize and viewed the need to do so as a sign of weakness. It served as a humorous reminder to me that sometimes I am like Fonzie. I know what needs to be said, but I choke on the words and often can't quite spit them out.

There are things we say that may hurt or offend, but there are also things that can be hurtful when we *don't* say them. In contrast, a person who is truly seeking to emulate the Savior will not only exclude harmful, hurtful garbage words but will also include words and phrases that heal wounds, such as "I'm sorry," and "Forgive me," and words of simple kindness, courtesy, and goodness, such as "Please," "Thank you," and "Excuse me." Such are included in the vocabulary of Christlike communication.

For he that will love life, and see good days,
let him refrain his tongue from evil, and his
lips that they speak no guile.
—1 Peter 3:10

5

That which the world calls righteousness
I have not any regard for.
To be righteous is to be just and merciful.
If a man fails in kindness, justice,
and mercy he will be damned.
—The Prophet Joseph Smith

Living the Golden Rule

Treating Others with Kindness and Consideration

I first became acquainted with Joe in the eighth or ninth grade. He had an epileptic seizure in our biology class. The teacher handled things very well and got Joe the help he needed, but the rest of the class was a little shocked by the experience. As is typical with many teenagers, especially when they don't understand something very well, some of the students refused to sit by Joe or be near him in the halls, because they were afraid that he might have another seizure. There were cruel jokes and merciless teasings behind Joe's back.

Over the months Joe was ostracized more and more. Not only did he have a physical disorder that made him different from the other kids in school, but he didn't dress in the most stylish fashions and wasn't part of the "in crowd." Joe lived close to me, and some days as I walked to school he would run to catch up to me and ask to walk with me. What could I say? Some of my friends would tease me for being "best friends" with Joe. "If you hang around with him," they would cruelly say, "you'll end up having seizures at school too." I was always uncomfortable with these mean statements, even if they were done in jest. Yet I was not strong enough to rebuke my friends, nor was I kind enough to really be a friend to Joe. I must admit that sometimes I would try to hide from him so I wouldn't have to walk to school with him and hear the ribbings of my friends. I didn't want the "cool" kids to think I was like Joe or that I was hanging out with him. I wasn't mean to him like the others, but neither was I very caring about him. I guess I have to admit that I merely tolerated his walking to school with me.

A few years later, when we were in high school, Joe had a serious seizure and was hospitalized. He became ill with some life-threatening complications. I didn't know anything about his condition until one day after seminary class, when my teacher asked me to stay after to talk to him. I thought I was in trouble. Brother Risenmay told me that Joe was seriously ill in the hospital and that he thought it would be nice for some of the kids from school to go visit him.

"Why are you asking me? I hardly know Joe," I said to my seminary teacher.

"He said that he only had one friend in all of the school," Brother Risenmay continued. "And he said that that only friend is you, Brent."

I was so totally shocked that I didn't know what to say for several minutes. I just sat there and shook my head. *How could he say that?* I wondered to myself. *I hardly know him. I've tried to avoid him when I could. I've only walked to school with him a few times—and that was only when I couldn't escape.* These were the kinds of thoughts that were racing through my mind at that moment. I should have been flattered that Joe considered me his friend, but instead I was feeling mostly ashamed—ashamed of my feelings and that I hadn't been a better friend to this young man who desperately needed one at that time in his life.

I have thought of this experience many times through the years—I've been almost haunted by its memory. I was truly sorry that I had been so embarrassed to be seen with Joe and that I had been unwilling to be his friend. Yet I am thankful for the painful lesson that I learned—that no act of kindness, even if it is just a smile or a simple greeting, even grudgingly given, is wasted or goes unnoticed or unrewarded. My experience with Joe taught me that the world is full of people like him, people starved for kindness, people starved for acts of consideration and simple friendliness.

Kindness is one of the divine attributes of the Savior. Numerous scripture references testify of the "loving kindness" of the Lord (see Psalm 51:1; Isaiah 54:8; 63:7; 1 Nephi 19:9; 3 Nephi 22:8–10; D&C 133:52). We speak often of the Savior's love, but inherent in that perfect love is also his gentleness, kindness, and consideration of others. "Kindness is one of the choicest of gems in the coronet of Truth," declared President David O. McKay. "Christ's short life among men was replete with acts reflecting this divine principle. His kindness won the loving but repentant sinner of Magdala, inspired hope and regeneration in the life of the woman sentenced to be stoned to death, and filled gracious mothers' hearts with eternal gratitude as He gently and lovingly blessed their little ones. Thus, just as His strength and perfect faith inspired the hardy fishermen of Galilee, and compelled even rulers of the Jews to seek wisdom and guidance at His feet, so His kindness shed its rays upon those who were weak and tender, guiding them along the pathway to peace and salvation." (*Pathways to Happiness,* comp. Llewelyn R. McKay [Salt Lake City: Bookcraft, 1957], p. 149.)

The Savior's injunction to do the things "which ye have seen me do" (3 Nephi 27:21) applies not only to the "big" acts of righteousness and service that he demonstrated, but also to the "little" acts of kindness and concern, of tenderness and patience, as well. " 'Life is made up not of great sacrifices or duties,' " President McKay once quoted, " 'but of little things in which smiles and kindness and small obligations given habitually are what win and preserve the heart and secure comfort' " (in Conference Report, October 1956, p. 6). How can I be like the Savior if I am unwilling to treat others with the same respect and concern that he would? "Therefore all things whatsoever ye would that men should do to you, do ye even so to them: for this is the law and the prophets" (Matthew 7:12). This Golden Rule should be the guiding principle in our relationships with others. How closely we adhere to that admonition demonstrates how far we have come in our quest to become more like Christ.

While on my mission to Denmark, I was hit by a car while I was riding my bicycle. Fortunately I was not seriously injured (although I could have been), but my bike was crunched beyond recognition. The reaction of the driver of the car that hit me was most interesting. Instead of coming to my assistance, he immediately got out of his car and inspected it for any damage. After he had checked out his car, he came over to me and proceeded to chew me out, even though the accident had been entirely his fault.

I have thought many times how the reaction of the driver of that car characterized the natural man, in contrast to what the Savior would have done. I have wondered if the man would have reacted the same way if he had smashed into an expensive Mercedes instead of a bicycle. Would he have treated me differently if I had been his boss or an important government official rather than just a white-shirted, flip-chart-toting Mormon missionary? If I am seriously striving to be more like Jesus, my concern for and treatment of others would not depend on such things. Jesus would treat prince or pauper with the same level of kindness and consideration, and so should I.

I have seen members of the Church who are very active—who hold important leadership callings, conscientiously pay their tithing, read their scriptures every day, and attend the temple regularly—yet who are unkind, overly demanding, difficult, and impatient and insensitive to their employees, students, family members, or others around them. Perhaps each of us have known people, whether fellow workers, neighbors, ward members, or even family members, who make us want to hide when we see them coming, out of fear of what they might say and how they might treat us. I have known and worked with people around whom I had to walk on eggshells, as it were, because I never knew how they might react to anything I might say or do.

When I observe acts of unkindness, insensitive or inconsiderate comments, or any form of treatment of others that is antithetical to Christ's loving kindness, I should take inventory of my own heart and examine my own treatment of others. Do I treat my students or office help with less deference, patience, and kindness than I would my boss or a General Authority? Do I ever feel justified to be unkind or insensitive to those "under me" and yet would never act that way to those "over me"? What would Jesus do? Would he be kind and considerate to the important people who could "further his career" and be indifferent at best or inconsiderate at worst to all others? Of course not, and neither should we be. "Courtesy is not unusual conduct to be reserved for a special circle of friends or circumstances," Elder Marvin J. Ashton taught. "It is not a veneer to be put on for special social occasions or people. It is a way of life of tremendous significance, whether it be in the home, in the office, or on the highway. . . . We cannot justify or condone discourtesy regardless of friendship or situation." (*What Is Your Destination?* [Salt Lake City: Deseret Book Co., 1978], p. 110.)

Jesus declared that righteousness is not obtained without the "weightier matters of the law." He chastised the Pharisees as being hypocritical because they performed some acts of righteousness and yet failed to incorporate into their lives those weightier traits and characteristics of determined and devout discipleship. "Woe unto you, scribes and Pharisees, hypocrites!" he boldly declared. "For ye pay tithes of mint and anise and cummin, and have omitted the weightier matters of the law, judgment, mercy, and faith: these ought ye to have done, and not to leave the other undone." (Matthew 23:23.) Being nice and kind to others is at least as weighty on the scales of righteousness, if not more so, as is paying tithing or attending the temple. I cannot come to know and be like Christ and yet trample on the tender feelings of others. It is through simple kindness and consideration of all that I demonstrate these weightier matters of discipleship. "It is indeed remarkable that the nature of our dealings with our fellowmen will determine, in large measure, our status in the kingdom of heaven," stated Elder Mark E. Petersen. "We may attend to rites and rituals and yet overlook the weightier matters such as brotherly kindness, honesty, mercy, virtue, and integrity. Let us never forget that if we omit them from our lives we may be found unworthy to come into His presence." (In Conference Report, April 1977, p. 109.)

Several years ago, while I was standing in a line at the crowded

BYU Bookstore during its annual Christmas sale, I noticed that the cashier was new and was having a difficult time getting each of the transactions correct. She needed help several times, and the people in the line were getting impatient and irritated with the delays. Finally, when the young man who was ahead of me in the line had finished his transaction, he launched a verbal tirade against the young woman cashier. "Do you realize how long we have had to wait in this line because of you?" he shouted. "I have no patience for such incompetence!" He took his purchase and left the store, still muttering his complaints. I was embarrassed, as were the other people standing around. I could only imagine how hurt and humiliated the young cashier must have felt.

Rudeness, impatience, and a lack of concern for the feelings of others are characteristic of the natural man, never of the man or woman of Christ. Would I treat the Savior that way, even if I was having a bad day? Of course not! Yet, as the Savior declared, "Inasmuch as ye have done it unto one of the least of these my brethren, ye have done it unto me" (Matthew 25:40). Just as President Hunter admonished us to ask ourselves "What would Jesus do?" he also urged us to seek to emulate the Master in all aspects of our lives. Perhaps it would be well for me to remember that if my secretary really "goofs up" something important in my office, or someone cuts me off in traffic, or the copy center doesn't have my handouts ready when I need them for class. I could be more patient and kind if I recognized that how I react to others, especially under duress, determines to a large degree what kind of person I really am.

"To be righteous is to be just and merciful," the Prophet Joseph Smith declared. "If a man fails in kindness, justice, and mercy he will be damned." (*Words of the Prophet Joseph Smith,* comp. Andrew F. Ehat and Lyndon W. Cook [Provo, Utah: Religious Studies Center, Brigham Young University, 1980], p. 206.) With the words of the Prophet echoing in my mind, it might be well to ask myself, "How would I treat this person if my salvation were dependent upon it?" I may be slow, but I'm not stupid. If I would ask myself that question in all situations, I think most, if not all, of my tendencies toward unkind comments or treatment would be eliminated. If I am to become more like Jesus I must seek to be more kind, gentle, considerate, and sensitive to others, for Christ is the personification of all these virtues. One cannot possess the requisite Christlike characteristic of charity, the pure love of Christ, without also being patient and kind, for "charity suffereth long, and is kind" (1 Corinthians 13:4). "One who is kind is sympathetic and gentle with others," President Ezra Taft Benson taught. "He is considerate of others' feelings and courteous in his behavior. He has a helpful nature. Kindness pardons others' weaknesses and faults. Kindness is extended to all—to the aged and the young, to animals, to those low of station as well as the high." (In Conference Report, October 1986, p. 62.)

The world today seems to put a higher premium on characteristics such as assertiveness and toughness than it does on kindness, patience, or gentleness. It has almost become a virtue in some circles to be considered a tough boss, assertive, or demanding. Unfortunately, however, those characteristics are often synonyms for words like *rude, unkind, impatient,* and *insensitive*. The world demands results—product is more important than process, ends justify the means, success is the "be all and end all," regardless of what one must do to people along the way to attain it. These worldy philosophies would justify treating an employee unkindly, because we would rationalize that our impatience, curtness, or unkindness is needed to override any incompetence or weakness on the part of the employee. "Some think the only way to get even, to get attention or advantage, or to win is to bash people," Elder Marvin J. Ashton observed. "Oftentimes character and reputation and almost always self-esteem are destroyed under the hammer of this vicious practice." (In Conference Report, April 1992, p. 23.) What a contrast this worldy philosophy of bashing is to the "philosophy" stated by the Lord in the revelations:

> No power or influence can or ought to be maintained by virtue of the priesthood, only by persuasion, by long-suffering, by gentleness and meekness, and by love unfeigned;
>
> By kindness, and pure knowledge, . . .
>
> Reproving betimes with sharpness, when moved upon by the Holy Ghost; and then showing forth afterwards an increase of love toward him whom thou hast reproved, lest he esteem thee to be his enemy;

> That he may know that thy faithfulness is stronger than the cords of death.
>
> Let thy bowels also be full of charity towards all men. (D&C 121:41–45.)

This inspired declaration does not just provide guidance for priesthood leaders and for the governance of God's kingdom; but perhaps, more important, it is a call to overcome the world, the tendencies of the natural man, and the sophistries of the world, and to use instead only kindness, gentleness, persuasion, patience, and consideration in our dealings with our fellowmen. "So what is the antidote for this bashing that hurts feelings, demeans others, destroys relationships, and harms self-esteem?" asked Elder Ashton. "Bashing should be replaced with charity."

> *Charity* is, perhaps, in many ways a misunderstood word. We often equate charity with visiting the sick, taking in casseroles to those in need, or sharing our excess with those who are less fortunate. But really, true charity is much, much more.
>
> Real charity is not something you give away; it is something that you acquire and make a part of yourself. And when the virtue of charity becomes implanted in your heart, you are never the same again. It makes the thought of being a basher repulsive.
>
> Perhaps the greatest charity comes when we are kind to each other, when we don't judge or categorize someone else, when we simply give each other the benefit of the doubt or remain quiet. Charity is accepting someone's differences, weaknesses, and shortcomings; having patience with someone who has let us down; or resisting the impulse to become offended when someone doesn't handle something the way we might have hoped. Charity is refusing to take advantage of another's weakness and being willing to forgive someone who has hurt us. Charity is expecting the best of each other.
>
> None of us needs one more person bashing or pointing out where we have failed or fallen short. Most of us are already well aware of the areas in which we are weak. What each of us does need is family, friends, employers, and brothers and sisters who support us, who have the patience to teach us, who believe in us, and who believe we're trying to do the best we can in spite of our weaknesses. Whatever happened to giving each other the benefit of the doubt?

> Whatever happened to hoping that another person would succeed or achieve? Whatever happened to rooting for each other? (In Conference Report, April 1992, p. 24.)

Kindness and Consideration at Home

In the days surrounding final exams, my home phone rings off the hook. Usually the callers are students wanting to know if they can take the exam either early or late. Even after the exam has already been administered, I invariably get a call or two from students who have neglected to take it (I think I have heard every excuse ever conceived in the minds of students). And after grades have already been submitted, I sometimes get phone calls or visits from students who want me to change their grades for any number of reasons, some justifiable and others just ridiculous.

One day, after I had spent some time on the phone with a student who had gotten himself in a real predicament and who needed me to bail him out by allowing him to take the exam late, my wife made an interesting comment. "You are so patient, understanding, and accommodating to your students," she said. I thought it was a nice compliment, until she dropped the other shoe with the rest of her observation. "I wish you were that way with your own children."

I don't think she meant her comment to be hurtful or critical. I know she thinks I'm a pretty good dad, but her words gave me food for thought. Do I really treat my students or coworkers with greater respect and kindness than my own family? Am I more willing to overlook small faults or be patient and forgiving of mistakes in others than I am with my own wife and children? Is my public persona of kindness and consideration toward others different from my private persona?

Why do we ofttimes treat strangers with more gentleness and kindness than we do our own children? Why are we more patient with the shortcomings of others than we are of our spouse? Shouldn't it be just the opposite? Shouldn't we be more kind and considerate to those we love the most? The need for real

Christlike living is at least as great within the home, if not more so, as it is at work or even at church. "The affection and thoughtfulness required in the home," Elder Neal A. Maxwell wrote, "are no abstract exercise in love, no mere rhetoric concerning some distant human cause. Family life is an encounter with raw selfishness, with the need for civility, of taking turns, of being hurt and yet forgiving, and of being at the mercy of others' moods. Family life is a constant challenge, not a periodic performance we can render on a stage and then run for the privacy of a dressing room to be alone with ourselves. The home gives us our greatest chance, however, to align our public and private behavior, to reduce the hypocrisy in our lives—to be more congruent with Christ." (*That My Family Should Partake* [Salt Lake City: Deseret Book Co., 1974], p. 180.)

When I served as a bishop, there were times when members of the ward would confess serious transgressions they had committed or discuss dumb mistakes they had made that hurt others. Although there were times I became irritated with some, never did I make rude comments like "You're so stupid! How could you do such a thing?" or treat any of them with less respect or kindness because of their mistakes. In fact, more often than not, I felt greater compassion toward them. When they wanted to talk, I was never too busy or distracted to listen with undivided attention. When things did not go as well or as quickly as we sometimes planned, I was patient. I thought that is how the Good Shepherd would have treated his flock and that he would want me to do the same. Yet why is it that I sometimes forget that my own family are a part of his flock as well?

I am a shepherd to my family just as much as a bishop is a shepherd to his ward. "The most important of the Lord's work you will ever do," President Harold B. Lee often stated, "will be within the walls of your own homes" (*The Teachings of Harold B. Lee,* ed. Clyde J. Williams [Salt Lake City: Bookcraft, 1996], p. 280). Just as I would be tender and patient and kind with ward members or fellow workers, I need to remember President Lee's words when my teenage driver comes home with a speeding ticket or wrecks the car, or when one of the children does pull-ups on the towel rack and pulls the whole wall down. I must try to act with the same civility and kindness when my own children make mistakes as I did when ward members confessed to me as a bishop. I must remember even when I'm having a bad day at home that brotherly kindness is as much a requirement of the disciple of Christ as is faith or humility or diligence (see D&C 4:5–6).

Being a nice person is as much a Christian virtue as is sacrifice, honesty, or faithful endurance. In fact, enduring to the end, according to Elder Hartman Rector Jr., "means that we will hereafter—(1) Continue to repent. (2) Continue to forgive others for the rest of our lives. Perhaps there is one other thing we must do: (3) We must be nice! I do not believe there will be anyone in the celestial kingdom that is not nice (see D&C 31:9; 52:40)." (In Conference Report, October 1990, p. 98.) I will not be Christlike if I keep the law of chastity, read my scriptures daily, never say a lie, and always do my home teaching, yet fail to be kind to and considerate of others. These are the weightier matters of Christlike living that cannot be overlooked or neglected while we are working on the other attributes. "The measure of a man is not necessarily his title or his position," Elder Victor L. Brown testified, *"but rather how he treats others"* (in Conference Report, October 1989, p. 96; emphasis added). More often than we suspect, these weightier matters of kindness, patience, consideration—just being nice—touch the most lives and yield unsung and unseen dividends. As an anonymous writer once penned:

> I have wept in the night
> For the shortness of sight
> That to somebody's need made me blind;
> But I never have yet
> Felt a tinge of regret
> For being a little too kind.

"Be ye kind one to another," the Apostle Paul admonished (Ephesians 4:32). These simple words could do more for peace and happiness in the world than almost anything else. I cannot, by myself, bring peace to war-torn nations of the world or eradicate sickness or hunger. I am not smart enough to solve society's problems—I struggle with solving my own problems and helping my kids with their math. But I am convinced that the Golden Rule that Jesus taught, if really understood and fully lived by all, could literally change the world.

Therefore, all things whatsoever ye would that men should do to you, do ye even so to them, for this is the law and the prophets.
—3 Nephi 14:12

Jesus eased suffering not just by laying healing hands upon the afflicted, but also through simple acts of kindness and tender expressions of consideration. Multitudes followed him, not merely because of his profound teachings and his miracles but also because of his "loving kindness." His divine kindness was demonstrated in smiles, in words of encouragement, and by being gentle and considerate, caring, and kind. People loved to be near him to hear him teach, to see him heal, but also because he was so nice! The people of his day, as well as ours, hungered for kindness. Kindness is the forerunner of charity, the pure love of Christ. If I truly desire to know—to understand and experience—Christ's loving kindness, I must extend the same to those around me.

I want to be kind to ev'ryone,
For that is right, you see.
So I say to myself, "Remember this:
Kindness begins with me."
(Clara W. McMaster, "Kindness Begins with Me,"
in *Children's Songbook,* p. 145.)*

6

A new commandment I give unto you,
That ye love one another; as I have loved
you, that ye also love one another.
By this shall all men know that ye are
my disciples, if ye have love one to another.
—*John 13:34–35*

Love One Another

Hearts Touched by the Pure Love of Christ

Like all newlyweds, my wife and I had to go through a period of adjustment when we were first married. We loved each other deeply, but there were still many things to learn and to work out together. One of the great challenges for me was to learn how to communicate my feelings and express my love for my wife; sometimes what I perceived to be an expression of love was not always perceived the same way by Wendy.

For some reason, Sundays were the hardest days for my wife when we were first married. She cried almost every Sunday for the first several weeks of our "newlyweddom." I would hold her in my arms and assure her that I loved her and that I was so glad that she was my eternal companion. Then I would go rest on the couch while she fixed Sunday dinner. In fact, it was on one of these occasions when I came to a startling realization about my "expressions of love" and why my wife may have been crying. We had been given the book *You and Your Marriage* by Elder Hugh B. Brown as a wedding gift. I read aloud the following words as I lay on the couch and Wendy worked in the kitchen. The words came out of my mouth before I fully realized what I had read, so there was no skipping this part: "The husband lying on the couch in the front room, may shout to his wife in the kitchen and say, 'Honey, I love you,' " Elder Brown wrote, "but it would be much more convincing if he would express it by taking a dish towel or a broom to help a bit. Sometimes a man says to his wife, 'I love you,' but his conduct says more loudly, 'I love me.'" (*You and Your Marriage* [Salt Lake City: Bookcraft, 1960], pp. 98–99.)

This statement hit me like a ton of bricks. I thought I had been so comforting and loving, when in reality my expressions had been somewhat hollow and self-serving. I tried harder from that day to *show* my love for Wendy, but I still had much to learn. Sometimes I would even try to be romantic by giving her mushy cards or flowers or a heart-shaped box of candies (that I would usually eat myself). Wendy would appreciate the token expressions of love but often had to remind me that a greater expression of my love would be to watch the kids so she could go somewhere, or to vacuum, or to help with the household chores more. It didn't seem nearly as romantic to me—but it meant more to her. From her I learned an important lesson: Expressions of true love are often the most mundane and simple acts.

Through the years I have come to learn that not only is this principle important in our marriages and families, though it may be the most obvious and most needed in the home; it is also just as important in our relationships with others in our church service and in our dealings with our fellowmen. The Lord has commanded us to love all men, not just our spouse, parents, and children. "Thou shalt love the Lord thy God with all thy heart, and with all thy soul, and with all thy mind. This is the first and great commandment," Jesus taught. "And the second is like unto it, thou shalt love thy neighbour as thyself." (Matthew 22:37–39.) Whether it be loving God, loving our families, or loving our neighbors, the principle is the same: He does not love who does not show his love.

At the Last Supper the Savior issued a new commandment to his disciples, a commandment that would become the distinguishing characteristic of true disciples of Christ: "A new commandment I give unto you, That ye love one another; as I have loved you, that ye also love one another. By this shall all men know that ye are my disciples, if ye have love one to another." (John 13:34–35.) The ancient Israelites had been previously commanded to love God and their neighbors (see Deuteronomy 6:5; Leviticus 19:18). But now they were given a new commandment to do something more, something greater, more divine, more pure. The new commandment was found in the key phrase "as I have loved you." The Savior's charge to his disciples then and now was to love others with charity, which is the pure love of Christ (see Moroni 7:47). If I am to live this "new commandment"—to love others as Jesus loved—then I must ask myself, "How did the Savior love others?"

Nephi gave us a glimpse of what constitutes Christ's divine love: "He doeth not anything save it be for the benefit of the world; for he loveth the world, even that he layeth down his own life that he may draw all men unto him" (2 Nephi 26:24). Everything that Jesus did was done out of his perfect love for mankind. Numerous scripture references testify of his divine love, but it is interesting to note that there are no explicit accounts of Jesus verbally expressing it—that is, we never read of Jesus saying directly to his disciples, "I love you." Undoubtedly, Jesus, the Perfect Exemplar in all things, expressed love on many occasions and to many different people and groups. I believe it is for a purpose that the scriptures emphasize Christ's love as seen through his actions more than through his verbal expressions. He healed the afflicted, he lifted the downtrodden, he taught the spiritually hungry, he blessed, he touched, he wept, he served—he loved!

Let us not love in word, neither in tongue;
but in deed and in truth.
—1 John 3:18

Many years ago a vicious crime occurred in New York City that captured the attention of the world. A young woman was stabbed to death as people watched from their apartment windows. As the woman was screaming for help, many people came to the windows to see what was happening, and others actually got up and closed their windows to muffle her screams. No one, however, came to her assistance. The nation was shocked and outraged that her pleadings for help had fallen on deaf ears.

I have often wondered what I would have done in that situation. What would Jesus have done? I doubt any serious disciple of Christ could stand idly by and do nothing. And I certainly can't imagine the Savior going to the window upon hearing the screams and yelling to the woman, "I love you and care about you. Please call if you need anything," and then closing the window and going back to bed. Such a scenario is ridiculous, and such an expression of love and concern would indeed be empty. The offer to help, unaccompanied by actions, would be meaningless. Yet in some ways that is how we express our concern for our fellowman.

In a similar way, we welcome a new member of the ward by raising our hands as their membership records are read in sacrament meeting, referring to this symbolic gesture as "extending the hand of fellowship." How unfortunate it is when, after we have raised the hand of fellowship, we go on our way, not speaking to or befriending these new members. Just extending a symbolic hand of fellowship is no more true fellowship and brotherhood than is shouting out a window "I love you" to a person being violently attacked. Loving one another cannot be merely an expression of a feeling or emotion, whether it be from the pulpit, in meetings or quorums, in neighborhoods, and especially at home. Loving as Christ loved requires action more than emotion. Dr. M. Scott Peck, a noted psychiatrist and best-selling author, wrote that "love is not a feeling."

> Many, many people possessing a feeling of love and even acting in response to that feeling act in all manner of unloving and destructive ways. On the other hand, a genuinely loving individual will often take loving and constructive action toward a person he or she consciously dislikes, actually feeling no love toward the person at the time and perhaps even finding the person repugnant in some way.
>
> The feeling of love is the emotion that accompanies the experience of cathecting [or affection]. Cathecting . . . is the process by which an object becomes important to us. . . . The misconception that love is a feeling exists because we confuse cathecting with loving. . . . But it is possible to love without cathexis [affection] and

> without loving feelings, and it is in the fulfillment of this possiblity that genuine and transcendent love is distinguished from simple cathexis. The key word in this distinction is "will." I have defined love as the *will* to extend oneself for the purpose of nurturing one's own or another's spiritual growth. Genuine love is volitional rather than emotional. . . . The person has made a commitment to be loving whether or not the loving feeling is present. If it is, so much the better; but if it isn't, the commitment to love, the will to love, still stands and is still exercised. (*The Road Less Traveled* [New York: Simon and Schuster, 1978], pp. 116–17, 119.)

The new commandment that Jesus gave his disciples was a charge to *do,* not just *feel.* Someone insightfully observed, "Love without service, like faith without works, is dead!" The Savior was commanding his disciples and us as well, to reach beyond themselves and to lift, strengthen, heal, comfort, encourage, and befriend—to serve one another. It may be impossible for us in mortality to possess the same feelings that Jesus has for mankind, because he is divine and we are mortal. However, we can serve others after the pattern the Savior gave us, and in so doing we will become possessors to some degree of the feelings of love the Savior has. Christlike love extends beyond our feelings of like or dislike, our prejudices, and our cultural or religious differences. It was this kind of love and service of which the Savior spoke when he responded to the question "Who is my neighbor?" or in other words, "Who is deserving of my love?" His response was in the form of a parable—the parable of the Good Samaritan (see Luke 10:25–37). In this parable Jesus rebuked the hypocritical Jews who, by virtue of their status as chosen people, had a greater responsibility to serve and bless others but who had failed to practice divine love. As the parable figuratively portrayed, they had "passed by on the other side" and pretended not to see the man in need. I believe that Jesus was teaching us that if we are to love and serve like him, we must remove whatever social, emotional, or spiritual blinders that prevent us, consciously or unconsciously, from recognizing those around us who need our love—our wilful actions of service, our words of encouragement, our hand of fellowship. "Those we serve, we love," Elder Robert L. Backman declared (in Conference Report, October 1985, p. 16).

We talk a great deal in the Church about service. We have service projects for the youth. Priesthood quorums have service projects at the welfare farm and help the widows of the ward. Relief Society sisters render considerable compassionate service such as taking meals into homes of the sick or after a baby is born. Home and visiting teachers render similar service to their assigned families. All of this is good and should not be neglected. Such service is an important function of the institutional Church. It is like a spiritual glue that binds us together. The great blessing of such priesthood-directed service is powerfully illustrated in the following experience recounted by Les Goates. During the terrible Spanish influenza or "black plague" epidemic of 1918, which took more than 14 million lives worldwide, the Goates family of Lehi, Utah, came to know in a most poignant way how love and service can ease the pain of suffering:

> Winter came early that year and froze much of the sugar beet crop in the ground. My dad and brother Francis were desperately trying to get out of the frosty ground one load of beets each day which they would plow out of the ground, cut off the tops, and toss the beets, one at a time, into the huge red beet wagon and then haul the load off to the sugar factory. It was slow and tedious work due to the frost and the lack of farm help, since my brother Floyd and I were in the army and Francis, or Franz, as everybody called him, was too young for the military service.
>
> While they were thusly engaged in harvesting the family's only cash crop and were having their evening meal one day, a phone call came through from our eldest brother, George Albert, . . . bearing the tragic news that Kenneth, nine-year-old son of our brother Charles, . . . had been stricken with the dread "flu," and after only a few hours of violent sickness, had died on his father's lap; and would dad please come to Ogden and bring the boy home and lay him away in the family plot in the Lehi Cemetery.
>
> My father cranked up his old flap-curtained Chevrolet and headed for Five Points in Ogden to bring his little grandson home for burial. When he arrived at the home he found "Charl" sprawled across the cold form of his dear one, the ugly brown discharge of the black plague oozing from his ears and nose and virtually burning up with fever.

"Take my boy home," muttered the stricken young father, "and lay him away in the family lot and come back for me tomorrow."

Father brought Kenneth home, made a coffin in his carpenter shop, and mother and our sisters, Jennie, Emma, and Hazel, placed a cushion and a lining in it, and then dad went with Franz and two kind neighbors to dig the grave. . . .

The folks had scarcely returned from the cemetery when the telephone rang again and George Albert . . . was on the line with another terrifying message: Charl had died and two of his beautiful little girls—Vesta, 7, and Elaine, 5—were critically ill, and two babies—Raeldon, 4, and Pauline, 3—had been stricken.

Our good cousins, the Larkin undertaking people, were able to get a casket for Charl and they sent him home and in a railroad baggage car. Father and young Franz brought the body from the railroad station. . . .

Next day my sturdy, unconquerable old dad was called on still another of his grim missions—this time to bring home Vesta, the smiling one with the raven hair and big blue eyes.

When he arrived at the home he found Juliett, the grief-crazed mother, kneeling at the crib of darling little Elaine, the blue-eyed baby angel with the golden curls. Juliett was sobbing wearily and praying: "Oh, Father in heaven, not this one, please! Let me keep my baby! Do not take any more of my darlings from me!"

Before father arrived home with Vesta the dread word had come again. Elaine had gone to join her daddy, brother Kenneth, and sister Vesta. And so it was that father made another heartbreaking journey to bring home and lay away a fourth member of his family, all within the week.

The telephone did not ring the evening of the day they laid away Elaine nor were there any more sad tidings of death the next morning. . . .

After breakfast dad said to Franz, "Well, son, we had better get down to the field and see if we can get another load of beets out of the ground before they get frozen in any tighter. Hitch up and let's be on our way."

Francis drove the four-horse outfit down the driveway and dad climbed aboard. As they drove along the Saratoga Road, they passed wagon after wagon-load of beets being hauled to the factory and driven by neighborhood farmers. As they passed by, each driver would wave a greeting: "Hi ya, Uncle George," "Sure sorry, George," "Tough break, George," "You've got a lot of friends, George."

On the last wagon was the town comedian, freckled-faced Jasper Rolfe. He waved a cheery greeting and called out: "That's all of 'em, Uncle George."

My dad turned to Francis and said, "I wish it was all of ours."

When they arrived at the farm gate, Francis jumped down off the big red beet wagon and opened the gate as we drove onto the field. He pulled up, stopped the team, paused a moment and scanned the field, from left to right and back and forth—and lo and behold, there wasn't a sugar beet on the whole field. Then it dawned upon him what Jasper Rolfe meant when he called out: "That's all of 'em, Uncle George!"

Then dad got down off the wagon, picked up a handful of the rich, brown soil he loved so much, and then in his thumbless left hand a beet top, and he looked for a moment at these symbols of his labor, as if he couldn't believe his eyes.

Then father sat down on a pile of beet tops—this man who brought four of his loved ones home for burial in the course of only six days; made caskets, dug graves, and even helped with the burial clothing—this amazing man who never faltered, nor flinched, nor wavered thoughout this agonizing ordeal—sat down on a pile of beet tops and sobbed like a little child.

Then he arose, wiped his eyes with his big, red bandanna handkerchief, looked up at the sky, and said: "Thanks, Father, for the elders of our ward." (Quoted by Elder Vaughn J Featherstone in Conference Report, April 1973, pp. 46–48.)

I have seen numerous lives blessed through the service of brothers and sisters of wards and stakes throughout the Church. Compassionate service blesses the giver as well as the receiver. It is a formalized means of showing, by loving and serving one another, that we are indeed Christ's disciples. For this reason, service projects will always be an integral part of the Church, a means whereby we "bear one another's burdens, that they may be light" and "mourn with those that mourn; yea, and comfort those that stand in need of comfort" (Mosiah 18:8–9). But these service projects may in some ways be part of the "lesser law" which, like the law of Moses, is a schoolmaster designed to lead us to something higher, something more lasting—serving and loving others in a more Christlike manner. Institutional service projects are like training wheels on a bicycle: They help us to be able to someday ride on our own and render individual service, consisting of personal concern, compassion, and acts of kindness and love that come from deep within one's own soul, not from a sign-up list. "I fear some members suffer from action paralysis," Elder Glenn L. Pace observed, "waiting for the Church to put its stamp of approval on one organization or another. The Church teaches principles. Use those principles and the Spirit to decide which organizations you would like to support."

> The Lord said, "Verily I say, men should be anxiously engaged in a good cause, and do many things of their own free will" (D&C 58:27). Good things can be done through the Church organization, community organizations, and very often through no formal organization at all.
>
> We must reach out beyond the walls of our own church. In humanitarian work, as in other areas of the gospel, we cannot become the salt of the earth if we stay in one lump in the cultural halls of our beautiful meetinghouses. We need not wait for a call or an assignment from a Church leader before we become involved in activities that are best carried out on a community or individual basis.
>
> When we get emotionally and spiritually involved in helping a person who is in pain, a compassion enters our heart. It hurts, but the process lifts some of the pain from another. We get from the experience a finite look into the Savior's pain as He performed the infinite atonement. Through the power of the Holy Ghost, a sanctification takes place within our souls and we become more like our Savior. We gain a better understanding of what was meant when He said, "Inasmuch as ye have done it unto one of the least of these my brethren, ye have done it unto me" (Matthew 25:40). (In Conference Report, October 1990, p. 10.)

Fulfilling Christ's new commandment to love as he has loved us requires more than just involvement in service. It requires charity, the pure love of Christ. It is this divine love that is the distinguishing characteristic of true discipleship. True charity is more than just service. Well then, how do I get charity? If it is not found in its fulness in quorum projects or Relief Society compassionate service, where is it to be found and obtained? "Pray unto the Father with all the energy of heart, that ye may be filled with this love," the prophet Mormon declared, "which he hath bestowed upon all who are true followers of his Son, Jesus Christ" (Moroni 7:48). If I am to be a true follower of Christ, I must pray for charity, the pure love of Christ, and it will come as a spiritual gift.

I must admit that in the past I think I have misunderstood this passage and the process described therein. I have usually thought of charity as a feeling that I would get from the Lord that would cause me to so powerfully and profoundly love everyone around me that I would then love and serve others as Jesus did. For some, it may actually come in that manner, but for me I have come to understand that the *feeling* of "the pure love of Christ" comes later, sometimes long after the *action* of charity. In seeking for this kind of Christlike love, what then should I pray for? I believe that instead of praying for an emotion to motivate us, we should pray for increased sensitivity and perception—the ability to recognize others' needs and to perceive what can and should be done, and then the courage to act upon that knowledge. It doesn't take much spiritual sensitivity or perceptiveness to recognize the "big needs" of others and the obvious service that can be done. Christlike love and service enables us to see the "small things" that are needed to touch hearts. If I am to become a true disciple of Christ, one who is sincerely seeking to be more like the Savior, I must love and serve out of my own heart and will, not just because of an assignment or a sense of obligation. It must come from within me. Charity, the pure love of Christ, is what I *am,* not just what I *feel.* Service must become a part of my very soul and character, not just something I do. Each expression of love and act of service, whether great or small, becomes a part of my character.

A few years ago I injured my back and was bedridden with a seriously herniated disc in my spine. It was too painful to get out of bed and get dressed. My family was taking good care of me and there really wasn't any glaring need in our home. If my home teachers would have called and asked if there was anything that could be done, I would have appreciated their call but probably would have told them there was nothing they could do. My neighbor, however, didn't call to ask. He just came over and mowed my lawn and didn't say a word about it. He wasn't my home teacher or quorum leader. He hadn't been assigned or even volunteered for the project. I had older children, or even my wife, who could have mowed the lawn, but my neighbor did it just as a friend. This man, who often thinks he's not very religious, was truly filled with charity, the pure love of Christ. It was a simple thing, but it touched my heart. He was Christlike simply because he showed his concern with a quiet act of service, not because he had to or even because he had thought much about it, but just because that's the way he is. To me, that is loving others as Christ loves. When we perceive a need, we don't even have to think much about it; we just do something that demonstrates our love and lifts the burdens of others. This friend is an example to me of true Christian discipleship. He may not be in the limelight in ward or stake leadership, but his simple acts of kindness, which are just part of his character, are more valuable than most other things we call service. Perhaps the Apostle Paul said it best:

> Though I speak with the tongues of men and of angels, and have not charity, I am become as sounding brass, or a tinkling cymbal.
>
> And though I have the gift of prophecy, and understand all mysteries, and all knowledge; and though I have all faith, so that I could remove mountains, and have not charity, I am nothing.
>
> And though I bestow all my goods to feed the poor, and though I give my body to be burned, and not charity, it profiteth me nothing. . . .
>
> Charity never faileth: but whether there be prophecies, they shall fail, whether there be tongues, they shall cease; whether there be knowledge, it shall vanish away. . . .
>
> And now abideth faith, hope, charity, these three; but the greatest of these is charity. (1 Corinthians 13:1–3, 8, 13.)

I am touched by the examples of prophets of God who, despite their enormous responsibilties and public service, demonstrate Christlike charity by simple, quiet, sometimes even anonymous acts of love. These private and simple acts of compassion bespeak what kind of disciples they really are. President Howard W. Hunter, who was one of the most gentle and Christlike men ever to bless the earth, often demonstrated by his simple dealings with others the pure love of Christ that filled his soul. Elder Neal A. Maxwell tells of an experience he had with President Hunter as they traveled together on a Church assignment to the Middle East. Since they shared a hotel room, Elder Maxwell, who was exhausted from their hectic schedule, asked President Hunter if it would be all right if he took a quick nap before their next appointment. After thirty minutes or so, Elder Maxwell awoke to the image of President Hunter sitting on the edge of his bed polishing Elder Maxwell's shoes. Elder Maxwell perceived that President Hunter was embarrassed that he had been caught in the act, for he would rather not have had Elder Maxwell even notice what he had done. Such a simple act speaks volumes of what he was really like. An Apostle shining the shoes of his beloved junior companion is a modern-day example of the Master washing the dusty feet of his disciples to demonstrate that "he that is greatest among you shall be your servant" (Matthew 23:11).

Many years ago President Kimball noticed a young mother with a crying child in the ticket line at an airport. The mother had been stranded in the airport by bad weather, and she had been trying for hours to get another flight. Two months pregnant and in danger of miscarrying, she had been warned by her doctor not to pick up her child; and so, to the criticism of the other travelers, she was trying to move her child along with her foot. President Kimball could tell how frustrated, fatigued, and harried this woman was, so he comforted her child, made arrangements for the pair to be put on another flight, and gave the woman words of encouragement, leaving only when assured she would be fine. Although there were many others around—worried about their own flights and luggage, all concerned about self—it was a quiet, gentle, Christlike elderly man, unknown to this woman, who helped her by literally lifting her burdens. (See Edward L. Kimball and Andrew E. Kimball Jr., *Spencer W. Kimball* [Salt Lake City: Bookcraft, 1977], p. 334.) It may not have seemed like much, and certainly President Kimball didn't have to think long and hard about what to do. He perceived a "little need" that meant so much to someone else. His perceptiveness and sensitivity evidenced his Christlike character. Elder Loren C. Dunn tells another story about President Kimball's quiet charity:

> A few years ago, President and Sister Spencer W. Kimball were touring missions overseas. A change in the airline schedule found them, along with a mission president and his wife, in a cold and

> drafty airport, late at night, with no place to go and nothing to do but wait for an early morning flight. Sister Kimball had her coat, but the mission president's wife did not. President Kimball tried to give her his coat, but she would not take it. As they began to fall asleep on those hard benches, President Kimball got up and gently put his coat over the sleeping wife of the mission president.
>
> This kind of selfless concern for others is how President Kimball lived his life. He literally spent his life in taking off his coat, so to speak, and putting it around the shoulders of those he judged to be in greater need: people of all colors and creeds; men, women, and children. It never made any difference to him. All were his brothers. All were his sisters. ("The Gospel of Love," in *Love* [Salt Lake City: Deseret Book Co., 1986], pp. 37–38.)

As I seek to emulate the Master—to love others as he would love them—I must conscientiously seek to remove the blinders from my eyes, whether those blinders be selfishness, shyness, laziness, preoccupation with my own needs and problems, or just not knowing what to do. As I take advantage of the institutional opportunities for service, I must also look for individual needs and seek to do something each day that extends me beyond myself, whether it is a simple act of friendship, a smile, a telephone call to someone who is lonely, or taking a meal (or flowers, cookies, or some other thing) to someone with no apparent need, just to say I care. As I seek to do these "little things" and as I continue to pray for charity and for sensitivity and perception of need, love and service become a natural part of me. I don't have to be constantly thinking, *Now, what can I do to love as Jesus loved?* It will begin to be second nature; or, more appropriately, it becomes part of my divine nature.

Proportionate with these actions of charity, the feelings of love, compassion, and concern will naturally follow. I will find myself caring more and feeling more love. It is this combination of feeling and wilful action that becomes the pure love of Christ: Not only do I feel Christlike love for others and perceive them as Christ perceives them, but I also feel Christlike love from the Savior. I feel his divine love for me and gain an even greater appreciation for his supreme, selfless service to mankind. Then, in a small but powerful way, I understand what is meant by the phrase "As I have loved you."

Love at Home

One Monday evening our youngest daughter asked, "What are we going to do for family home evening tonight?"

"We're going to have a service project," I answered.

"That sounds fun," Janie responded. "Where are we going to go and what are we going to do?"

"We're not going anywhere," I told her. "We're going to stay right here and do service for our family."

Janie looked at me like I was crazy, and then said what she was thinking: "That's not a service project. You can't do service in your own home—that's work!"

My daughter's reaction to the idea of "family service" I think typifies a common misconception. Almost always when we think of the Savior's charge to "love one another as I have loved you," or when we think of service or the meaning of the parable of the Good Samaritan, we tend to think of loving and serving our fellowmen—those outside the scope of our immediate view. Yet the principles that I have already discussed have just as much application, if not more, to our own families. Speaking to parents, King Benjamin admonished them in their family responsibilities:

> And ye will not suffer your children that they go hungry, or naked; neither will ye suffer that they transgress the laws of God, and fight and quarrel one with another, and serve the devil, who is the master of sin, or who is the evil spirit which hath been spoken of by our fathers, he being an enemy to all righteousness.
>
> But ye will teach them to walk in the ways of truth and soberness; *ye will teach them to love one another, and to serve one another.*
>
> And also, ye yourselves will succor those that stand in need of your succor; ye will administer of your substance unto him that standeth in need. (Mosiah 4:14–16; emphasis added.)

Service Within the Family

I believe that if we as parents will teach our children within the walls of our own homes by precept and example, and by allowing them to experience for themselves the blessings and joy of serving one another, it will become a part of their very character.

The home is the most important laboratory for the cultivation of all Christlike virtues. From the home the effects of love and service can then ripple outward and bless others.

The principle of love being volitional rather than emotional is perhaps best illustrated within the family. I don't think I am alone in admitting that there are times when I may know that I love the members of my family, but I have to convince myself that I like them. I'm sure my kids and my wife on a given occasion feel the same way. It is at these times that love becomes an act of will, not a feeling. "The person who has earned love the least," observed Elder F. Enzio Busche, "needs it the most" (in Conference Report, April 1982, p. 98). If I truly desire to be more like the Savior, I must be willing to be at least as sensitive and perceptive of the needs of my family as I am to my fellowmen. Perhaps the times when I feel the least like serving or doing something that would evidence my love for a family member are the very times when I should take off the blinders and reach out to them, even if they initially repel my expression of love or acts of sincere service.

One of the frustrations I feel as a parent comes from trying to get my children to do nice things for each other. For example, one of the kids will demand of a brother or sister, "Will you please [I use the word *please* even though more often than not the word is not in my children's vocabulary] get your clothes out of the dryer so I can put mine in?" For some reason it doesn't dawn on them that they could take them out and put them in the laundry basket themselves—maybe even fold them nicely too. One of the all-too-common expressions in our home is "That's not my job!" I get frustrated when we become so compartmentalized in our job descriptions that we see only our own responsibilities. I can't imagine the Savior seeing a need but then shrugging it off, saying, "It's not my job." I am not saying that we should do everything for our kids, nor am I suggesting that we not teach responsibility and self-reliance. I am suggesting, however, that labeling things as "wife's work," "husband's job" (I don't know what that would be except to watch over the remote control to the TV), or "kids' job" sometimes is a way of putting on blinders that prevent us from reaching beyond ourselves and showing our love for others by doing something that would lift their burdens a little. Such "little things," especially when done anonymously, are often met with surprise and maybe even shock at first, then appreciation; and soon such little acts of service within the family begin to perpetuate themselves. I cannot force my children to be more sensitive, thoughtful, loving, and giving to one another, but I can teach them and I can lead the way. I can at least try to be more to my family like Jesus was to others (see Ephesians 5:22–33).

The Prophet Joseph Smith, despite his many responsibilities to the Church and the heavy demands placed upon him, always sought to love and serve his family. One of his contemporaries, Jesse W. Crosby, recounted an interesting encounter with the Prophet that taught him the importance of service within the family:

> Some of the home habits of the Prophet—such as building kitchen fires, carrying out ashes, carrying in wood and water, assisting in the care of the children, etc.—were not in accord with my idea of a great man's self-respect. [The Prophet coming to my house carrying a sack of flour he had borrowed] gave me the opportunity to give him some corrective advice which I had desired to do for a long time. I reminded him of every phase of his greatness and called to his mind the multitude of tasks he performed that were too menial for such as he; to fetch and carry flour was too great a humiliation. "Too terrible a humiliation," I repeated, "for you who are the head, and you should not do it."
>
> The Prophet listened quietly to all I had to say, then made his answer in these words: "If there be humiliation in a man's house, who but the head of that house should or could bear that humiliation?"
>
> Sister Crosby was a very hardworking woman, taking much more responsibility in her home than most women take. Thinking to give the Prophet some light on home management, I said to him, "Brother Joseph, my wife does much more hard work than does your wife."
>
> Brother Joseph replied by telling me that if a man cannot learn in this life to appreciate a wife and do his duty by her, in properly taking care of her, he need not expect to be given one in the hereafter.
>
> His words shut my mouth as tight as a clam. I took them as terrible reproof. After that I tried to do better by the good wife I had

> and tried to lighten her labors. (In *They Knew the Prophet,* comp. Hyrum L. Andrus and Helen Mae Andrus [Salt Lake City: Bookcraft, 1974], p. 145.)

Service begins at home. If I am to be more like the Savior in loving and serving others, that character trait must be nourished within my own family. "What would the Savior do?" must be as significant a guiding and governing principle in my relationships with my wife and children as it is in my relationships with others. Loving others as Christ loved us—expressing it by deeds as well as words—is truly a family affair, for we are all family: Whether moms or dads, brothers or sisters, sons or daughters, or even strangers, we are the family of God.

Expressing Our Love to Family Members

Love without action is not real love, but expressing that love in words is also vital to strengthening relationships and touching hearts. When I was in my first year of college I was deeply moved by a talk I heard at a general priesthood meeting I attended in the Tabernacle. I was impressed by the Spirit to make a long-distance telephone call to my parents in Idaho to express to them my love and appreciation.

It was late at night when I returned to my dorm room and made the call. My father was rather concerned when he heard my voice so late at night. "I just called to say I love you," I said. After a brief pause, my dad's response was, "Did you wreck the car or do you just need money?" When I convinced him that I really did just call to express my love and appreciation, there was an even longer pause. Then, his voice cracking with emotion, my father said, "We love you too." It made me realize how rare my expressions of love had been and how much they meant to my parents.

I know a young husband who almost prides himself on not verbally expressing love to his wife. He thinks it is a clever joke and a funny way to tease her. "Do you love me?" his wife will ask. "I married you, didn't I?" is his response. While it is true that actions speak louder than words, it sure is nice to hear the words too. I am reminded of the scene in *Fiddler on the Roof* where the father, Tevye, asks his wife, "Golda, do you love me?" The song that follows demonstrates the need for both words and deeds in showing love. Golda recounts in her song all the things that she has done for him through their decades of marriage: cooking his meals, darning his socks, bearing his children. "But do you love me?" Tevye asks again. I am touched by the song because it reminds me that all of us—even when we know that we are loved and can see the active evidence of that love—need to hear verbal assurances of love.

The volitional deeds of concern and service we do to show our love are like the sunshine, soil, and water that are essential to the growth of a tender plant. The sincere expressions of love that we say within our homes, such as "I love you," "I am proud of you," " I am so thankful for you," and "You mean so much to me," are like fertilizer. The nutrients stimulate good growth and deep roots, and help to keep the plants healthy and productive.

> I think when I read that sweet story of old,
> When Jesus was here among men,
> How he called little children like lambs to his fold;
> I should like to have been with him then.
>
> I wish that his hands had been placed on my head,
> That his arms had been thrown around me,
> That I might have seen his kind look when he said,
> "Let the little ones come unto me."
> (Jemima Luke, "I Think When I Read That Sweet
> Story," in *Children's Songbook,* p. 56.)

When I think of "that sweet story of old," I can almost see the Savior putting his arms around not only little children but also others who needed his healing hugs. I can visualize him holding Mary and Martha close as they wept together at the loss of their beloved Lazarus. I can almost hear him expressing his love, as well as his compassion, to the blind and the lame and the deaf. There must have been tender expressions of love at the Last Supper and as he walked with his disciples to Gethsemane. Although the scriptures emphasize his loving actions, I am convinced that those deeds were always accompanied by loving words.

The scene and the circumstances may be different today, but the charge to "love one another as I have loved you" is the same. What would Jesus do? I think I know the answer, and it is his example I want to follow. When it comes to love at home, I need to "show and tell" more—to show my love with deeds and to accentuate it with words. I can help my wife with the housework more, but also hold her tight and tell her more often how much I love her and how much she means to me. I can show my love for my children by helping them with their homework or science projects (or, heaven forbid!—building a pinewood derby race car). I can teach them how to make their jump shots and how to dribble behind their backs. I can show them I love them by going to their activities, even if they lose the game or their violins squawk at the concert. But I can also hug them more and tell them how thankful I am that Heavenly Father sent them to me. I might have to hold them a little tighter at times when they don't want my hugs, but I need to say "I love you" more often than I do. What a difference it would make in the lives of our families if our spouse and children didn't have to wonder and certainly never had to ask, "Do you love me?"

Motivating by Love

"I have loved thee with an everlasting love," the Messiah declared in the book of Jeremiah, "therefore with lovingkindness have I drawn thee" (Jeremiah 31:3). The word ***drawn*** means "invite," "urge," or "motivate." "I drew them," the Lord told the prophet Hosea, "with bands of love" (Hosea 11:4). The Savior loves us so much that if we can feel of his perfect love we are drawn to him and motivated to pattern our lives after him. "If we could feel or were sensitive even in the slightest to the matchless love of our Savior and his willingness to suffer for our individual sins," Elder David B. Haight taught, "we would cease procrastination and 'clean the slate,' and repent of all our transgressions" (in Conference Report, April 1988, p. 26). There was no bullying or intimidation on the part of the Savior. People followed him and kept his sayings not out of fear, but out of love—love for him fostered by his love for them. "You cannot drive people to do things which are right," President George Albert Smith taught, "but you can love them into doing them" (in Conference Report, April 1946, p. 185). The more I feel of Christ's love and mercy in my life, the more I am drawn to him; the more I desire to live his teachings and to have others feel that love in their own lives.

In a similar manner, I find it insightful that Lehi, after he had his dream of the tree of life, sought to motivate his own family not with "hellfire and damnation" lectures or intimidation, but rather "he did exhort them then with all the feeling of a tender parent" (1 Nephi 8:37). Such is a Christlike approach to leadership, whether in our homes or in the Church. The Savior was not the Good Shepherd because he dragged his sheep to the fold, but because he called each one by name, taking them into his arms if necessary to carry them to safety (see John 10:1–15). Loving and leading are really related. A person may lead without love, but there will be no willing followers. "Nothing is so much calculated to lead people to forsake sin as to take them by the hand, and watch over them with tenderness," the Prophet Joseph Smith instructed. "When persons manifest the least kindness and love to me, O what power it has over my mind, while the opposite course has a tendency to harrow up all the harsh feelings and depress the human mind." (In *History of the Church* 5:23–24.) The following experience demonstrates how love is a powerfully motivating force:

> I remember when I first earned my license to drive. I was about sixteen, as I recall. I'd been driving off and on for three years (scary thought, isn't it?). My father had been with me most of the time during my learning experiences, calmly sitting alongside me in the front seat, giving me tips, helping me know what to do. My mother usually wasn't in on those excursions because she spent more of her time biting her nails (and screaming) than she did advising. My father was a little more easygoing. Loud noises and screeching brakes didn't

bother him nearly as much. My grandfather was the best of all. When I would drive his car, I would hit things . . . *Boom!* He'd say stuff like, "Just keep on going, Bud. I can buy more fenders, but I can't buy more grandsons. You're learning." What a great old gentleman. After three years of all that nonsense, I finally earned my license.

I'll never forget the day I came in, flashed my newly acquired permit, and said, "Dad, look!" He goes, "Whoa! Look at this. You got your license. Good for you!" Holding the keys to his car, he tossed them in my direction and smiled, "Tell you what, son . . . you can have the car for two hours, all on your own." Only four words, but how wonderful: "All on your own."

I thanked him, danced out to the garage, opened the car door, and shoved the key into the ignition. My pulse rate must have shot up to 180 as I backed out of the driveway and roared off. While cruising along "all on my own," I began to think wild stuff—like, *This car can probably do 100 miles an hour. I could go to Galveston and back twice in two hours if I averaged 100 miles an hour. I can fly down the Gulf Freeway and even run a few lights. After all, nobody's here to say "Don't!"* We're talking dangerous, crazy thoughts! But you know what? I didn't do any of them. I don't believe I drove above the speed limit. In fact, I distinctly remember turning into the driveway early . . . didn't even stay away the full two hours. Amazing, huh? I had my dad's car all to myself with a full gas tank in a context of total privacy and freedom, but I didn't go crazy. Why? My relationship with my dad and my granddad was so strong that I couldn't, even though I had a license and nobody was in the car to restrain me. Over a period of time there had developed a sense of trust, a deep love relationship that held me in restraint. (Charles R. Swindoll, *The Grace Awakening* [Dallas: Word Publishing, 1990], pp. 47–48.)

If we are to lead and love others as the Lord did, we too must motivate by love, or charity, "the pure love of Christ." Righteousness is not obtained out of guilt, embarrassment, humiliation, or fear. While these attitudes may induce temporary change, it is only through the pure love of Christ that enduring change and spiritual transformation are obtained.

Love Is Its Own Reward

Several years ago I was given one of the most challenging home teaching assignments I have ever had. However, it was through this assignment that I gained some of the greatest insights into the true meaning of the Savior's charge to "love one another as I have loved you." I was assigned to a family that had not been active in the Church for over twenty years. The parents of the family were older than my own parents; in fact, they had grandchildren closer to my age. They had been married in the temple nearly fifty years earlier but had never been back. To make matters worse, the father had been recently excommunicated and was extremely bitter toward the Church and the stake leaders. I'm still not sure why I was allowed to visit them, since he would not allow any other visitors from the Church.

My first visit was rather awkward—I had never met these people before. I had not been fully prepared for that visit, and I was astonished at what I saw. The little old home was quite run down. The place was filthy, and I wasn't quite sure where to sit—or even if I should sit down. They had a grown son living with them who helped them take care of another adult son who was severely mentally and physically handicapped. I didn't know anything about all of this, and I was immediately shocked by the sights, sounds, and smells that I encountered.

At first I would make my monthly visit and we would talk about the weather, gardens, and just about anything that did not remotely relate to the Church or the gospel. Then I started dropping in on them as I walked to and from work, just to say hi and to see how things were going. Pretty soon I was making contact with them several times a week, not because I really planned it that way, but I found that I enjoyed visiting with them. After not many visits, I didn't notice the things that had repulsed me at first.

I took my children to visit them, and almost immediately they became friends with the handicapped son and starting calling my home-teaching family "Grandma and Grandpa Perkins," "Uncle Bob," and "Uncle Richard." What started out as an assignment to love became much more. I found that I loved being with them. I gained far more than I gave. Yes, I got them to a few ward activities and even to sacrament meeting a few times over a period of several years, but there was no immediate prospect for reactivation or for Grandpa Perkins's rebaptism. But that was secondary. I reached out a little to them, and the initial acts of service and concern were soon swallowed up by charity, the pure love of Christ. I got more sincere love from them than I ever could have imagined.

On one occasion I became ill with a bad cold and missed a few days of work and didn't visit them. Before I could call or set up a home teaching appointment, they came to visit me. Their concern for and service to their home teacher was more than anything their home teacher gave in return. In the wintertime they brought firewood to our family. At Christmas there were presents under the tree from them to each of our children. They shared more meaningful gospel messages with me through their examples of sincere appreciation and genuine love than my "canned messages" brought to them.

After five years as their home teacher, to the outside observer it may have appeared that things had not changed much. But it was I who had changed. I had experienced the pure love of Christ with what I felt for them and with what I felt and received from them. The parable of the Good Samaritan meant more to me than ever. I had seen a family labeled inactive, who had become alienated from others and were looked down upon by many, "bind up my wounds" and care for me by taking me into their hearts. I went from being just a home teacher trying to do my duty to being like a son and a brother. My feeble efforts to love them were rewarded a hundred times over. Love is its own reward.

I wish there were a storybook ending to this experience. The family still isn't active in the Church. But a few years after I had moved away from that community, I went back to that home-teaching family to see how they were doing. There were hugs and tears of joy. "Grandpa Perkins" had had a leg amputated and was now nearly blind, yet he recognized my voice as soon as I entered their home. Before I left, he said, "Brent, when I come back into the Church, will you baptize me?" Unfortunately he died before that day ever came, but—love is its own reward.

The Savior commands us to "love one another as I have loved

you" not so much just for the good we can do for others here on earth or for the eternal reward that we may someday inherit, though each of these are by-products of love. I believe that Jesus desires us to love one another so that we may come to partake of the fruit of the tree of life—the pure love of Christ—"the most desirable above all things" (1 Nephi 11:22). We come to know God through loving and serving his children. We come to taste of the sweetness of Christ's love, that which is "most joyous to the soul" (1 Nephi 11:23), through loving others, as he loves us. Charity, the pure love of Christ, is its own reward. My efforts to be more Christlike in my love and service to others will yield even greater dividends for me than what it does for others, for it changes me. Through the pure love of Christ I become a partaker of the divine nature (see 2 Peter 1:3–8). Loving others is in and of itself its own reward, for God is love.

Beloved, let us love one another: for love is of God;
and every one that loveth is born of God, and knoweth God.
He that loveth not knoweth not God; for God is love. . . .
Beloved, if God so loved us, we ought also to love one another.
. . . If we love one another, God dwelleth in us,
and his love is perfected in us.
—1 John 4:7–8, 11–12

7

I, even I, will both search my sheep, and seek them out. . . . I will feed my flock, and I will cause them to lie down, saith the Lord God. I will seek that which was lost, and bring again that which was driven away, and will bind up that which was broken, and will strengthen that which was sick.
—Ezekiel 34:11, 15–16

"Feed My Sheep"

Ministering to Others as the Good Shepherd Did

While my family lived in Israel we saw a lot of sheep and goats. In fact, a Bedouin family lived just on the other side of the hill from the Center, and I watched them every morning leading their flock to pasture and then leading them back home at the end of the day. I was fascinated by this shepherding and watched it closely, observing what the shepherd did and how the sheep responded to their master.

On the Judean hills between Jerusalem and Jericho I saw many sheep grazing on what little grass there was. It was always interesting to me to watch the Palestinian shepherds bring their flocks back home at sundown. They would lead them down the hill back to the camp, separating the goats from the sheep and leading each group into its separate "fold"—a pen or corral.

These images are indelibly planted in my memory. As I now read the scriptures, I have a greater appreciation for the shepherding imagery used by the Old Testament prophets and the Savior in the New Testament. This passage took on greater significance because of an experience we had there: "How think ye? if a man have an hundred sheep, and one of them be gone astray, doth he not leave the ninety and nine, and goeth into the mountains, and seeketh that which is gone astray? And if it so be that he find it, verily I say unto you, he rejoiceth more of that sheep, than of the ninety and nine which went not astray. Even so it is not the will of your Father which is in heaven, that one of these little ones should perish." (Matthew 18:12–14.)

After visiting the archaeological remains of the ancient city of Pella in modern-day Jordan, I walked with my class along the river to the road where the bus was to pick us up to take us to the next site. As was our practice, after we had loaded the bus I asked for the "bus captains" to report if everyone was on board and accounted for. With the assurance that all were there, we proceeded to drive to the next location. After about a half-hour, one of the students approached me and said, "Brother Top, I hate to tell you this, but we're missing somebody. John is not here."

"Are you sure?" I asked, hoping he had just overlooked John.

"Yes, I'm sure," Jack said. "We've checked the entire bus and he's not here." Then Jack took me back to where John had been sitting to show me the empty seat, John's scriptures and backpack—but no John.

I panicked and had the sickest feeling in my stomach. *How could we have left him behind?* I wondered. *How am I going to be able to explain this—that we just lost a student at an isolated site in the country of Jordan? What am I going to say to his parents?* There were a million things going on in my mind. I had the bus driver turn around—we had to go back and find John.

The students consoled me and assured me that everything would be all right, because everyone knows that if you get separated you should just stay where you are and people will come and get you. At least, so we thought. At that point the students quit worrying, thinking all we had to do was go back and pick up John. So they began to have fun and make the most of the situation. They began video-taping a "documentary" about John's disappearance. Another student made a sign that read, "Have you seen John?" and held it up in the front window of the bus in the view of passing motorists. Even our tour guide and bus driver got into the fun. Our bus driver would honk the horn and yell out his window in Arabic to people on the sidewalks and along the road, "Have you seen John?" People looked at us like we were crazy. We were laughing and having so much fun. Then these light-hearted feelings changed completely.

We returned to Pella and spread out over the site, shouting out for John—but all to no avail. John was nowhere to be found. When we boarded the bus, instead of laughing and joking about "our little lost lamb," there was a subdued silence. The seriousness of the situation was apparent to all, and we were now worried about John's safety. We went to the police station, but they knew nothing. We asked people in the village if they had seen an American tourist walking around. None had seen him. Whereas just moments earlier we were all laughing and the bus was filled with merriment, at that moment there was now a profound sense of concern. The silence was deafening. While our bus driver and guide were talking with the police and local merchants, we had class prayer and pleaded with the Lord for the safety of John and that we would be able to locate him soon. At the close of this heartfelt prayer, my wife reached out and squeezed my hand and assured me that everything would be all right. She knew by the power of the Spirit that our prayers had been heard.

In one last attempt to find John at the site where we had left him, our guide asked a group of men who were walking not far from where we last saw John if they had seen him. "Yes, we saw him. He said he had been left by his group, and he caught a ride with one of the villagers." Now all we could do was go on with our trip and hope that John caught up with us.

Several hours later, when our bus arrived at the archaeological site of Jerash, a Roman city from the time of Jesus, there was John, waiting for us in the entrance lobby of the visitor's center. Boy, were we glad to see him! We hugged him and rejoiced that he was safe and again part of our group. It was as if a cloud was lifted and we could now go back to laughing and joking and having a good time once again.

I am sure that my students and I will always remember this experience. "He was lost, and now he is found." No site that we visited that day, no new knowledge we learned about geography or history could compare in any way to what we learned about concern for each other and about what Jesus meant when he spoke of going out into the wilderness to find even one sheep that is lost. Despite the ulcer and gray hair that I earned during those frantic few hours, I have a greater appreciation for the Savior as the Good Shepherd.

> I am the good shepherd: the good shepherd giveth his life for the sheep.
>
> But he that is an hireling, and not the shepherd, whose own the sheep are not, seeth the wolf coming, and leaveth the sheep, and fleeth: and the wolf catcheth them, and scattereth the sheep.
>
> The hireling fleeth, because he is an hireling, and careth not for the sheep.
>
> I am the good shepherd, and know my sheep, and am known of mine.
>
> As the Father knoweth me, even so know I the Father: and I lay down my life for the sheep. (John 10:11–15.)

Ministering to the Flock of God

Jesus was a *minister,* not an *administrator,* and as such he is the role model for our leadership and service in the Church. He is, as the Apostle Paul wrote, the "great shepherd of the sheep" (Hebrews 13:20). The word *minister* comes from an old English word which means "servant"—one who provides sustenance and service to another. Related to *minister* is the word *pastor,* which comes from the Latin and means "shepherd." In this way, one who ministers must be like a shepherd who cares for, looks after, protects, and feeds the flock. As we serve and minister, or look after and provide nourishment and concern to one another, we must pattern our ministering after the example and teachings of the Good Shepherd. "When the Good Shepherd bade farewell to His disciples, important instructions were given," Elder Russell M. Nelson has taught.

> "Jesus saith to Simon Peter, Simon, son of Jonas, lovest thou me more than these? He saith unto him, Yea, Lord; thou knowest that I

love thee. He saith unto him, *Feed* my *lambs."* (John 21:15; emphasis added.)

Because the available manuscripts of the New Testament are in Greek, additional insight is gained when the meaning of the words italicized above are studied in the Greek language. In the preceding verse, the word *feed* comes from the Greek term *bosko,* which means "to nourish or to pasture." The word *lamb* comes from the diminuitive term *arnion,* meaning "little lamb."

"[Jesus] saith to him again the second time, Simon, son of Jonas, lovest thou me? He saith unto him, Yea, Lord; thou knowest that I love thee. He saith unto him, *Feed* my *sheep."* (Verse 16; emphasis added.)

In this verse, the word *feed* comes from a different term, *poimaino,* which means "to shepherd, to tend, or to care." The word *sheep* comes from the term *probaton,* meaning "mature sheep."

"[Jesus] saith unto him the third time, Simon, son of Jonas, lovest thou me? Peter was grieved because he said unto him the third time, Lovest thou me? And he said unto him, Lord, thou knowest all things; thou knowest that I love thee. Jesus saith unto him, *Feed* my *sheep."* (Verse 17; emphasis added.)

In this verse, the word *feed* again comes from the Greek *bosko,* referring to nourishment. The word *sheep* was again translated from the Greek term *probaton,* referring to adult sheep.

These three verses, which seem so similar in the English language, really contain three distinct messages in Greek:

- Little lambs need to be nourished in order to grow;
- Sheep need to be tended;
- Sheep need to be nourished.

Therefore, one of the tangible signs of the restored church of Jesus Christ would have to be the establishment of an orderly system by which each precious member—young or old, male or female—might be given the continuing care and nourishment the Lord decreed for every one of His flock. . . .

The Good Shepherd lovingly cares for all sheep of His fold, and we are His true undershepherds. Our privilege is to bear His love and to add our own love to friends and neighbors—feeding, tending, and nurturing them—as the Savior would have us do. By so doing, we evidence one of the godly characteristics of His restored Church upon earth. ("Shepherds, Lambs, and Home Teachers," *Ensign,* August 1994, pp. 16, 19.)

One of my favorite places where we took the students in Israel was a sheepfold in the countryside near Jerusalem. It still is used by Palestinian shepherds today, and was perhaps used by Jewish shepherds at the time of Christ and even earlier. Until I actually visited this place, I must admit that I didn't really understand the difference between a "flock" and a "fold." To me, the terms as I read them in the scriptures seemed synonymous. But seeing this place made the scriptures come alive. I could clearly see the distinction, and I was also taught another aspect of what it means to be an undershepherd among the sheep of the Good Shepherd.

A sheepfold is usually located near a rocky area with cliffs or ledges that serve as a protective backdrop to the fold. The *flock* is comprised of the actual sheep and lambs, whereas the *fold* is the structure or area where they are safely kept from the dangers of the outside world. There are often caves in the back of the rocky area where the shepherd can take the flock in bad weather. (It may have been in a sheepfold cave like this that the Savior was born. It certainly was in similar environs that angels jubilantly announced the birth of the Messiah to shepherds in the area of Bethlehem.) In the front of the area, usually in a semicircle, the shepherd stacks up a wall of rocks—and there are plenty of them in the Holy Land—to serve as an enclosure for the sheep. This rock wall is high enough that the sheep can't jump over it and escape from the fold. A gate or doorway is the entrance whereby the shepherd leads his flock out to pasture in the daytime and in to the safety of the fold at night. With the sheep "safe folded" together, the shepherd's job is one of watching over them and making sure that no wild animals attack the sheep or that no rustlers sneak into the fold and steal livestock. Sometimes several shepherds may safeguard their flocks together in the same fold. In the morning when the shepherds come to get their sheep, they call them by name; and each shepherd's sheep recognize his voice and follow him to pasture. These images were used by the Savior in his teaching of the disciples:

> Verily, verily, I say unto you, He that entereth not by the door into the sheepfold, but climbeth up some other way, the same is a thief and a robber.
>
> But he that entereth in by the door is the shepherd of the sheep.

> To him the porter openeth; and the sheep hear his voice: and he calleth his own sheep by name, and leadeth them out.
>
> And when he putteth forth his own sheep, he goeth before them, and the sheep follow him: for they know his voice.
>
> And a stranger will they not follow, but will flee from him: for they know not the voice of strangers. . . .
>
> Then said Jesus unto them again, Verily, verily, I say unto you, I am the door of the sheep. . . .
>
> I am the door: by me if any man enter in, he shall be saved, and shall go in and out, and find pasture.
>
> The thief cometh not, but for to steal, and to kill, and to destroy: I am come that they might have life, and that they might have it more abundantly.
>
> I am the good shepherd: the good shepherd giveth his life for the sheep. (John 10:1–5, 7, 9–11.)

With these symbols I think the Savior is also teaching us about being undershepherds among his sheep. The sheep could represent individual Church members, while the flock of Christ is his Church collectively. The fold could represent the institutional Church—its programs, quorums, and structure—all designed to protect and perfect the Saints. The fold has a valuable purpose in the protection of the sheep, but the shepherd must be more worried about his flock than he is about the fold. If he spends all of his time building up the walls of the fold, he may actually neglect the sheep and expose them to greater danger. There is a need for balancing the maintenance of the protective fold and vigilance over the precious flock. With these symbols the Lord may be reminding us that we, like Peter of old, are commanded to "feed my lambs," not "run my church." Ministering to the flock is more important than administering the fold. Ministering to people is needed more than merely administering programs. As undershepherds we must remember that ministering requires both feeding and protecting the sheep, or the Saints of God. "Take heed therefore unto yourselves, and to all the flock, over the which the Holy Ghost hath made you overseers," the Apostle Paul commanded the elders of the Church, "to feed the Church of God, which he hath purchased with his own blood" (Acts 20:28). What do we feed them and how can we protect them?

Feasting upon the Words of Christ

The mortal Messiah taught the Samaritan woman that those who drink of the water of Jacob's well "shall thirst again: But whosoever drinketh of the water that I shall give him shall never thirst; but the water that I shall give him shall be in him a well of water springing up into everlasting life." (John 4:13–14.) Later at the synagogue in Capernaum, Jesus declared that he had something to give the world even more nourishing and life-sustaining than the manna that was given to the ancient Israelites as they wandered in the wilderness. "Labour not for the meat which perisheth," he admonished the people, "but for that meat which endureth unto everlasting life, which the Son of man shall give unto you" (John 6:27).

> Then Jesus said unto them, Verily, verily, I say unto you, Moses gave you not that bread from heaven; but my Father giveth you the true bread from heaven.
>
> For the bread of God is he which cometh down from heaven, and giveth life unto the world.
>
> Then said they unto him, Lord, evermore give us this bread.
>
> And Jesus said unto them, I am the bread of life: he that cometh to me shall never hunger; and he that believeth on me shall never thirst. . . .
>
> I am the living bread which came down from heaven: if any man eat of this bread, he shall live for ever: and the bread that I will give is my flesh, which I will give for the life of the world. (John 6:32–35, 51.)

We as undershepherds, like the Good Shepherd, lead the sheep to green pastures where they can feed upon the good word of God. Our task is to get those to whom we minister to partake of the doctrines of the kingdom by teaching them the scriptures and leading them to experience the blessings of the Savior's atonement in their own lives. "Feast upon the words of Christ," Nephi declared (2 Nephi 32:3). We feed his lambs and nourish his sheep by giving them the "Bread of Life" and the "Living Waters." They feast upon the words of Christ both by studying the scriptures and the principles of the gospel and by experiencing the life-changing power of the word of God.

"True doctrine, understood, changes attitudes and behavior," Elder Boyd K. Packer has taught. "The study of the doctrines of the gospel will improve behavior quicker than a study of behavior will improve behavior." (In Conference Report, October 1986, p. 20.) True ministers to the flock of God feed them "knowledge and understanding" (Jeremiah 3:15) and "the strength of the Lord" (Micah 5:4). We cannot force-feed them, but we must lead them to the green pastures of Christ, where they can freely partake of that which sustains, strengthens, and saves. As the prophet Isaiah declared: "Come, my brethren, every one that thirsteth, come ye to the waters; and he that hath no money, come buy, and eat; yea, come buy wine and milk without money and without price. Wherefore, do not spend money for that which is of no worth, nor your labor for that which cannot satisfy. Hearken diligently unto me, and remember the words which I have spoken; and come unto the Holy One of Israel, and feast upon that which perisheth not, neither can be corrupted, and let your soul delight in fatness." (2 Nephi 9:50–51; see also Isaiah 55:1–2.)

If we are having problems with those we are called to lead, perhaps teaching them doctrines and gospel principles will have a more positive effect than teaching them organizational skills or trying to fix the problem with a Band-Aid approach of worldly self-help ideas and pop psychology.

Putting on the Armor of God

Since I was a child I have loved the story of David and Goliath. This Old Testament story has become even more real to me because of our living in Israel and the many times that I stood in the valley of Elah, slung some smooth stones at an imaginary Goliath, and read the scriptural account to my family and students. I have tried to visualize a young boy, maybe only twelve or thirteen years old, indignantly questioning the Israelite soldiers why none would fight this Philistine who taunted them and mocked their God. King Saul heard of David's words and sent for the boy, who declared to him, "Let no man's heart fail because of [Goliath]; thy servant will go and fight with this Philistine." Saul refused to let him go at first, even though neither he nor any of his men had yet found the courage to face Goliath; saying, "Thou art not able to go against this Philistine to fight with him: for thou art but a youth, and he a man of war from his youth" (1 Samuel 17:32–33). But David assured Saul that the Lord would protect him, and thus the king consented.

I have tried to imagine how silly David must have looked when Saul placed his own armor and helmet upon the young shepherd from Bethlehem. It was bad enough that Saul was allowing him to go down to battle Goliath, but it would be worse not to adequately protect him. David probably couldn't even walk, let alone raise a sword, because of the weight and bulkiness of the armor. "I can't wear this," David may have said. "I must use the weapons I am used to." So he took off the armor, picked up his sling, and chose five smooth stones and put them in his shepherd's bag; and as he walked down the hill to meet Goliath in the valley, he was transformed from a boy to a man—a man of God.

> And the Philistine came on and drew near unto David; and the man that bare the shield went before him.
>
> And when the Philistine looked about, and saw David, he disdained him: for he was but a youth, and ruddy, and of a fair countenance.
>
> And the Philistine said unto David, Am I a dog, that thou comest to me with staves? And the Philistine cursed David by his gods.
>
> And the Philistine said to David, Come to me, and I will give thy flesh unto the fowls of the air, and to the beasts of the field.
>
> Then said David to the Philistine, Thou comest to me with a sword, and with a spear, and with a shield: but I come to thee in the name of the Lord of hosts, the God of the armies of Israel, whom thou hast defied.
>
> This day will the Lord deliver thee into mine hand; and I will smite thee, and take thine head from thee; and I will give the carcases of the host of the Philistines this day unto the fowls of the air, and to the wild beasts of the earth; that all the earth may know that there is a God in Israel.
>
> And all this assembly shall know that the Lord saveth not with sword and spear: for the battle is the Lord's, and he will give you into our hands. (1 Samuel 17:41–47.)

The great message of this story is found in the fact that David understood that his protective power was not in his stone-slinging skills, but in the strength of the Lord. He did not need Saul's armor, not just because it didn't fit but because he was protected by something far greater—the armor of God.

As we minister to the flock of God today, we too must instill in them the faith of young David and clothe them with the protective power of the armor of God. A shepherd cannot keep his sheep forever in the safe confines of the fold. Eventually he must lead them to pasture, even though there may be unseen dangers present. In a similar way, we as undershepherds cannot *isolate* those to whom we have the responsibility to minister from all of the temptations and trials of the world, "for there must needs be opposition in all things" (2 Nephi 2:11). But we can *insulate* them from the "fiery darts of the wicked" (Ephesians 6:16) by the protective influence of the Lord. How can we do that? The Lord himself has given us the answer:

> Wherefore, lift up your hearts and rejoice, and gird up your loins, and take upon you my whole armor, that ye may be able to withstand the evil day, having done all, that ye may be able to stand.
>
> Stand, therefore, having your loins girt about with truth, having on the breastplate of righteousness, and your feet shod with the preparation of the gospel of peace, which I have sent mine angels to commit unto you;
>
> Taking the shield of faith wherewith ye shall be able to quench all the fiery darts of the wicked;
>
> And take the helmet of salvation, and the sword of my Spirit, which I will pour out upon you, and my word which I reveal unto you, and be agreed as touching all things whatsoever ye ask of me, and be faithful until I come, and ye shall be caught up, that where I am ye shall be also. (D&C 27:15–18.)

Only through a steady diet of the word of God—the scriptures, doctrines, and spiritual experiences—can the flock of God be filled with truth, faith, and the Spirit. These characteristics create much-needed protection in the world today. Bomb shelters, automatic weapons, and even seventy-two-hour kits cannot replace the protective coating of the armor of God, for it is more powerful than any other thing we can do to insulate the flock of God from the evil of the day. As Alma learned in ministering to his own people: "And now, as the preaching of the word had a great tendency to lead the people to do that which was just—yea, it had had more powerful effect upon the minds of the people than the sword, or anything else, which had happened unto them—therefore Alma thought it was expedient that they should *try the virtue of the word of God*" (Alma 31:5; emphasis added).

Ministering to Our Families

The most important flock that needs our ministering, or our spiritual nourishing and protection, is found within the walls of our own homes. The Good Shepherd condemns being an effective leader in the Church or a conscientious undershepherd to others' families while neglecting our own. Even the Prophet Joseph Smith, his counselors in the First Presidency, and the bishop of the Church were rebuked of the Lord for their neglect. They had overlooked the most important work of a true shepherd—to feed and protect one's own lambs. "You have not kept the commandments, and must needs stand rebuked," the Lord declared unto the Prophet. "Your family must needs repent and forsake some things, and give more earnest heed unto your sayings." (D&C 93:47–48.) These prominent Church leaders, including the Prophet himself, were under condemnation because their families were not in order (see D&C 93:41–50). Despite all of the good work they were performing to build up the kingdom of God and bless Church members, the Lord commanded them to "set in order your own house, for there are many things that are not right in your house" (D&C 93:43). We are certainly not exempt today from this command, which is the primary commandment given by the Good Shepherd to all his undershepherds—to "first set in order thy house" (D&C 93:44).

> And again, inasmuch as parents have children in Zion, or in any of her stakes which are organized, that teach them not to understand the doctrine of repentance, faith in Christ the Son of the living God,

> and the baptism and the gift of the Holy Ghost by the laying on of the hands, when eight years old, the sin be upon the heads of the parents.
>
> For this shall be a law unto the inhabitants of Zion, or in any of her stakes which are organized.
>
> And their children shall be baptized for the remission of their sins when eight years old, and receive the laying on of the hands.
>
> And they shall teach their children to pray, and to walk uprightly before the Lord. (D&C 68:25–28.)

Several research studies have been conducted in recent years that have demonstrated the paramount importance of setting in order our homes by teaching our children to "feast upon the words of Christ" (2 Nephi 32:3) and to "put on the whole armour of God" (Ephesians 6:11). These studies have shown that all Church activities, programs, and efforts are handicapped if there is neglect of proper ministering at home. As a result, the Church has made program changes to strengthen the family, such as the consolidated meeting schedule and the new budget policy, with its accompanying effect on activities and Church programs. The Church is teaching by example and counsel that what the Lord needs is not more effective Church leaders or better programs or activities, as valuable as these are; but rather, stronger families. We need better parents more than we need better Primary teachers or bishops. Feeding and protecting the flock within our own homes will yield greater dividends than devoting all of our energies to administering programs, planning activities, or running the Church. "The home is the basis of a righteous life," declared Elder Harold B. Lee. "With new and badly needed emphasis on the 'how' [of Church programs], we must never lose sight of the 'why' we are so engaged. The priesthood programs operate in support of the home, the auxiliary programs render valuable assistance. . . . Both the revelations of God and the learning of men tell us how crucial the home is in shaping the individual's total life experience. . . . Much of what we do [in the Church] organizationally, then, is scaffolding, as we seek to build the individual, and we must not mistake the scaffolding for the soul." (In Conference Report, October 1967, p. 107.)

If we truly believe J. E. McCulloch's statement often quoted by President David O. McKay, "No other success can compensate for failure in the home," and if we are truly seeking to follow the example of the Good Shepherd, we will dedicate our greatest shepherding efforts to our own families (see J. E. McCulloch, *Home: The Savior of Civilization* [Washington, D.C.: The Southern Co-operative League, 1924], p. 42). It is certainly counterproductive to seek to solve problems in priesthood quorums and Relief Societies and in the meantime create future problems by failing to protect our own families in providing them with a gospel-centered, scripturally founded, testimony-building, spiritual environment. "When the real history of the world is fully disclosed," Elder Neal A. Maxwell asked, ". . . will what happened in cradles and kitchens prove to be more controlling than what happened in congresses?" (In Conference Report, April 1978, p. 14.) Perhaps we could paraphrase Elder Maxwell's words to also say, "What happens in family rooms, backyards, and around the kitchen table may prove more soul-shaping and problem-solving than what happens in the bishop's office or the cultural hall."

Over the last few years I have been involved in conducting a study, in connection with the Center for the Studies of the Family at Brigham Young University, among nearly five thousand Latter-day Saint youth in different parts of the United States, from the East Coast to Utah County to the Pacific Northwest. We have been investigating how these youth's religious beliefs and practices help deter delinquency. The results have provided us with valuable insight into not only how we can better minister to the youth of the Church but, most important, what families can do to spiritually clothe their children in the protective armor of God. More important than mere activity in the Church, the spiritual dimensions of the home and family—how the family helped these young people experience and internalize the principles of the gospel—were the most significant factors in protecting our youth from the many dimensions of delinquency. (See Brent L. Top and Bruce A. Chadwick, "Rearing a Righteous Family in a Wicked World," *This People,* Fall 1995, pp. 18–26; see also "The Power of the Word: Religion, Family, Friends, and Delinquent Behavior of LDS Youth," *BYU Studies* 33, no. 2 [1993], pp. 293–310.)

These results empirically demonstrate what the prophets and Apostles have consistently taught us. The home is where the flock of God is best nurtured and nourished on the words of Christ and where the armor of God is most effectively forged. "The ministry of the prophets and Apostles leads them ever and always to the home and family," President Boyd K. Packer explained. "That shield of faith is not produced in a factory, but at home in a cottage industry. The ultimate purpose of all we teach is to unite parents and children in faith in the Lord Jesus Christ."

> The plan designed by the Father contemplates that man and woman, husband and wife, working together, fit each child individually with a shield of faith made to buckle on so firmly that it can neither be pulled off nor penetrated by those fiery darts.
>
> It takes the steady strength of a father to hammer out the metal of it and the tender hands of a mother to polish and fit it on. Sometimes one parent is left to do it alone. It is difficult, but it can be done.
>
> In the Church we can teach about the materials from which a shield of faith is made: reverence, courage, chastity, repentance, forgiveness, compassion. In church we can learn how to assemble and fit them together. But the actual making of and fitting on of the shield of faith belongs in the family circle. Otherwise it may loosen and come off in a crisis. . . .
>
> This shield of faith is not manufactured on an assembly line, only handmade in a cottage industry. Therefore our leaders press members to understand that what is most worth doing must be done at home. Some still do not see that too many out-of-home activities, however well intended, leave too little time to make and fit on the shield of faith at home. (In Conference Report, April 1995, p. 8.)

Ministering Within the Church

Several years ago while I was serving as high priests group leader in my ward, I had an experience that once again reminded me of the true meaning of ministering within our callings in the Church. The wife of a member of the quorum was bedridden with a serious heart disease. She hadn't been able to attend church meetings in many years. Her visiting teachers would call her regularly but visit only sporadically, and the home teachers most often visited with her husband after church. I asked if I could bring my wife and visit her on Sunday and administer the sacrament to her. She was thrilled, for in all those years she had not had the priesthood leaders offer to bring her the sacrament.

When we visited I understood better why some had been previously afraid to visit her—she had two very large, intimidating dogs that were always near her bed. My initial reaction was to get out of there as soon as possible with all my arms and hands and feet still intact, but instead I prayed for protection from the dogs and then proceeded to visit with her and administer the sacrament. It was one of the best things I did in that calling. I'm not sure what it did for her, but it taught me a great lesson. She held my hand and thanked us profusely for coming to visit her. It meant so much to her, and with tears streaming down her face she told me that I was the first priesthood leader to visit her since she became so sick. "Why is that?" I asked. "Oh, because they are so busy," she replied. "I couldn't expect them to come and visit, because they have so many meetings to attend and so many things to look after in the ward and stake." She was sincere in saying that she did not expect visits from ward or stake leaders "because they are so busy."

I think her comments reflect a common problem: We sometimes become so busy administering programs that we don't have time to minister to people. In my leadership experiences in the Church—in bishoprics, on high councils, even as bishop—I discovered that much of what we "stew about" in our meetings and what causes the most stress in our callings has more to do with administration than ministration; more with programs, meetings, agendas, and plans than feeding and protecting the flock of God through personal, inspired ministering. I believe that the Good Shepherd would want us to seriously consider the following questions as we take inventory of our own efforts to lead like the Savior:

—Do we really know the flock to which we are undershepherds? Do we visit their homes? Do we know their names?

Do we really know their needs and innermost feelings and desires?

—Do we really understand that people are more important than programs? Do we utilize the programs of the Church and adapt them as needed to bless people, rather than making people fit the programs?

—Do we really believe that we serve to save souls, not merely to seek statistics?

—Do we express sincere love and appreciation for those to whom we minister? Do we love and serve without expectation? Would we continue to minister even if we don't see progress or if our love and concern are not reciprocated?

—Are we patient with our flock? Do we recognize individual differences in spiritual progress and maturity? Do we understand that some of our sheep are spiritual late bloomers and need our attention longer than others?

—Is our shepherding more spiritually based than socially motivated? Do we teach the gospel in our service? Do we use the scriptures in our counseling? Do we bear our testimony? Do we seek to find ways for our flock to feel the Spirit and know the love of God?

The work of an undershepherd in the Church is the same as in the home. Ministering requires feeding the flock the spiritually sustaining words of Christ and protecting the sheep from the wolves of the world by vigilance and by helping to outfit them in the armor of God. Programs and activities that are designed only to increase activity do not have the power to save. Such things may be fun and interesting, but like a steady diet of desserts, they will leave those we serve malnourished, weak, and vulnerable to spiritual sickness or attacks from the adversary. Similarly, activities and programs that do not teach the doctrines of the kingdom, that don't lead to true spiritual experiences, and that are not faith- and testimony-building opportunities may be socially appealing to some, but not spiritually sustaining or protective against "the fiery darts of the adversary" (1 Nephi 15:24).

In the previously cited study that was conducted among nearly five thousand LDS youth, we learned that neither activity in the Church as measured by attendance statistics alone nor social acceptance in the ward had sufficient power to counteract the negative influences of peers. What emerged as significant factors in empowering these youth to resist temptations were their own private religious behaviors, such as engaging in personal prayer, scripture study, and so on; and their own personal spiritual experiences—feeling the Spirit in their lives and seeing the gospel in practical action. The more these youth engaged in these faith-building activities and the more they felt a personal closeness to God in their lives, the less they engaged in immoral behaviors and other acts of delinquency.

As this study empirically demonstrated, protection against the wickedness of the world is not found in programs or exciting activities. Rather, modern prophets have consistently taught that we must not only teach the truths of the gospel to those to whom we minister, but also lead them to experience the fruits of the Spirit in their own lives. President Spencer W. Kimball admonished Church leaders and teachers to increase their efforts in assisting not only the youth of the Church but also all the Saints with whom they serve to more fully experience the gospel and more inwardly feel its spiritual benefits in their lives. "You are not merely to teach lessons or expound doctrine or set up tools and prescribe programs," he counseled. "Your success is not only in setting up ideals but in motivating [the Saints] to put these ideals into their lives." ("Circles of Exaltation," in *Charge to Religious Educators,* 2d ed. [Salt Lake City: The Church of Jesus Christ of Latter-day Saints, 1981], p. 10.) This is the kind of ministering that nourishes as well as protects the flock from the dangers that lie beyond the safe confines of the fold. The dangers are not always seen but are still combatted the same way the persuasive power of Lucifer was overcome in the premortal war in heaven: "And they overcame him by the blood of the Lamb, and by the word of their testimony" (Revelation 12:11). "To meet the difficulties that are coming," President Heber C. Kimball prophesied, "it will be necessary for you to have a knowledge of the truth of this work for yourselves. The difficulties will be of such a character that the man or woman who do not possess this personal knowledge or witness will fall. . . . The time will come when no man or woman will be able to endure on borrowed light. Each will have to be guided by the light within himself. If you do not have it, how can you stand?" (As quoted in Orson F. Whitney, *The Life of Heber C. Kimball,* 2d ed. [Salt Lake City: Bookcraft, 1945], p. 450.)

On the Mount of Olives, only days before his death, the Savior taught his disciples concerning the signs of the last days that would precede his second coming. "For in those days there shall also arise false Christs, and false prophets, and shall show great signs and wonders," he prophesied, "insomuch, that, if possible, they shall deceive the very elect, who are the elect according to the covenant" (Joseph Smith–Matthew 1:22). He then gave the prescription for protection against such deception in the last days: "And whoso treasureth up my word, shall not be deceived" (verse 37). That is the work of modern-day ministers in the kingdom of God—to lead the flock to the green pastures of the Good Shepherd, where they can freely treasure up his words and be protected by the shield of faith in him.

"He Must Increase, but I Must Decrease"

There are many things we can do to emulate the Savior in our service and love for the sheep of his flock, but there are also things we cannot do. I can feed and protect his sheep, but only he can save them. For that reason not only should our leadership and service in the Church incorporate Christlike qualities of compassion, concern, and love, but we could also pattern our leadership after John the Baptist. He recognized that although his mission was important, there were still things that only the Master could do. "Ye yourselves bear me witness, that I said, I am not the Christ, but that I am sent before him," John declared to his own disciples. "He that hath the bride is the bridegroom: but the friend of the bridegroom, which standeth and heareth him, rejoiceth greatly because of the bridegroom's voice: this my joy therefore is fulfilled. He must increase, but I must decrease." (John 3:28–30.) John's mission was to prepare the way for the Messiah (see Isaiah 40:3; Matthew 3:3). His teachings were to prepare the hearts of his listeners for the greater message of Christ. Therefore, he gladly directed his disciples to the Master and testified of his divinity. There was no competing for popularity or for disciples. He fully understood that his role was to lead souls to Christ, not to stand in their way or distract them from the Lord's saving power.

As undershepherds we must remember that we, like John, are to prepare the way. We can feed, nurture, teach, and strengthen, but only the Good Shepherd can change hearts, bring forgiveness, spiritually transform, and ultimately save. We do not seek to bring disciples to ourselves. We do not overstep our stewardship by seeking to be surrogate parents or bishops, and certainly never surrogate saviors. We lead the sheep and lambs to whom we are to minister to those relationships that are most important and, in turn, to the Good Shepherd. As his undershepherd I can lead them to the green pastures, but he alone is the Bread of Life (see John 6:35). I can direct them through precept and example to walk "beside the still waters," but Jesus is the Living Waters of which they must drink to eternally quench their thirst (see Psalm 23). We can follow his admonition to "feed my lambs," but in all our ministering and serving we must remember that the Lord Jesus Christ is "the Shepherd and Bishop of [our] souls" (1 Peter 2:25).

Feed the flock of God which is among you,
taking the oversight thereof, not by constraint, but willingly;
not for filthly lucre, but of a ready mind;
neither as being lords over God's heritage,
but being ensamples to the flock.
And when the chief Shepherd shall appear, ye shall receive
a crown of glory that fadeth not away.
—1 Peter 5:2–4

8

Wherefore, ye must press forward
with a steadfastness in Christ,
having a perfect brightness of hope,
and a love of God and of all men.
Wherefore, if ye shall press forward,
feasting upon the word of Christ,
and endure to the end, behold,
thus saith the Father:
Ye shall have eternal life.
—2 Nephi 31:20

ALWAYS REMEMBER HIM

Pressing Forward with a Steadfastness in Christ

I have a friend from Virginia who was an exceptional baseball player in his younger years. While he was serving as bishop of his ward, I heard him share the following experience from his playing days that impressed me deeply at the time. I believe it teaches a valuable lesson for us today.

My friend's high school team was playing in the state championship game, and he was the starting pitcher. His performance in that most important game of his life could be characterized by common sports metaphors such as "He had his best stuff" or "He was in a zone," meaning he was pitching flawlessly. The opposing team's batters vainly flailed at his rising fastball. He hadn't pitched very long until it was apparent that something special was occurring—he had struck out every batter he faced. His fastball had never been better, and his pitch location was pinpoint accurate. Every inning soon became an instant replay of the previous one—

three batters and three strikeouts, each batter helpless against my friend's overpowering fastball.

In the top of the seventh, the last inning of this championship game, my friend's team was on the verge not only of winning a state championship but of doing so in a historic manner, with a pitcher who was truly having a perfect game. The first batter of the inning met the same fate of the previous eighteen batters; he swung wildly at three straight fastballs. One out, two to go. The second batter took the first pitch. It was a hard fastball that tailed away from the hitter, catching the outside corner of the plate. "Strike one!" the umpire yelled. The next pitch, another hard fastball, was a little high, and the umpire yelled out something that had not been heard much in the game: "Ball one." The next two pitches were fastballs that the batter fouled off. Two strikes on the batter. One strike and one out away from a state championship and a perfect game.

My friend tried to be tricky with the next pitch and get the batter to swing at a curveball. His fastball had been so overpowering and had so dominated every batter who faced it that he thought, *This will get him for sure. I'll take something off this pitch and throw him a curveball. He'll be totally fooled!* The catcher gave the sign—one finger down meant fastball, but my friend shook off the sign. The catcher was shocked. To make sure, he gave the sign for the fastball again, and once again my friend shook his head. The catcher showed two fingers—the sign for an off-speed curveball. It would be the first time in the game that my friend threw any pitch other than a fastball. He went into his windup and delivered a slow breaking curve. It caught the batter and everybody in the stands by surprise. The batter had just enough time to adjust slightly and fouled the ball off.

My friend's coach immediately came running from the dugout to the pitcher's mound. "What in the ——— are you doing throwing that pitch?" the coach angrily shouted at his pitcher. "Are you crazy?"

"I thought I could fool him with a change-up or a curveball," my friend tried to explain. "Look, coach, he barely got a piece of it. I'll get him on the next pitch."

"I don't want to see another curveball or change-up in this game," the coach demanded. "You stick with your best stuff. Your fastball has been awesome today. Don't let up!"

My friend couldn't understand why his coach was so upset. He had thrown one curveball and it resulted in a harmless foul ball. He wondered if his coach would have still been angry with him for throwing a curveball if he had struck the batter out.

On the next pitch he threw a powerful fastball right past the batter. "Strike three. You're outta there!" the umpire shouted. Two outs. One out away from a championship.

The next batter stepped into the batter's box. It was the last chance to ruin a no-hitter and perfect game. Winning the game was now out of the question for the opposing team, but they hoped to at least get a hit. My friend fired two straight fastballs right past the batter for strikes. They were so blazing fast that the batter couldn't even get the bat off his shoulder before the ball was past him. The batter barely made contact with the next pitch, another fastball, and fouled off. Another fastball. Another foul ball. Another fastball and another foul ball. The catcher gave the familiar sign—fastball. My friend shook his head. He didn't want to throw another fastball. He wanted to get him with a change-up pitch. The catcher gave him the fastball sign again. My friend shook it off again. The catcher emphatically signalled fastball. This time my friend, thinking he knew best and that he was in complete control of all his pitches, disregarded the catcher's sign and the coach's previous warning: "I don't want to see another curveball or change-up." He threw what he considered to be the perfect change-up, but the batter got just enough of the ball to hit a slow rolling grounder to the second baseman. The throw to first base was easy. The game was over. He did it—he had thrown a no-hitter and a perfect game (no one had even reached first base), and his team had won the state championship. What a feeling! He was mobbed by his teammates and fans, but the coach wouldn't even speak to him.

After the celebration had subsided and the players were back in the locker room, the coach approached the jubilant winning pitcher. "How could you be so stupid?" the coach disgustedly declared. "I told you not to throw that pitch again. You threw it all away with that stupid change-up!" The coach was so angry that he was red in the face.

My friend couldn't understand why the coach would react that way—they had won the championship and he had pitched a perfect game. "Why are you so upset?" my friend asked. "We won and I pitched a perfect game—not one batter even got to first. How can you say that I threw anything away?"

"You don't get it, do you?" the coach responded. "You could have pitched the truly perfect game—you could have attained something that no one could ever top. You were one pitch away from having struck out every batter you faced—the ultimate perfect game. But you let up for one pitch, and it cost you." With that, the coach shook his head and walked away. My friend sat silently, realizing what the coach meant. If only he hadn't disobeyed his coach and let up on that one pitch.

I have thought how striving to be like the Savior is like attempting to pitch a perfect game. It is a daunting challenge and discouraging at times. It requires our "best stuff," and we cannot afford to let up. Sometimes in my attempt I struggle with the temptation to throw up my hands and let up or give up because I see how far I am away from the Ideal—the Perfect Exemplar. There is such a wide gap between where I am and where I want to be. It seems that just when I am cruising along toward my "perfect game," I stumble and fall. The natural man wants to let up, but the "Man of Christ" in me pushes me forward and reminds me that I must "press forward with a steadfastness in Christ" (see 2 Nephi 31:20). The phrase *press forward* implies "hanging on," "pushing forward," and "bearing down." It requires dogged determination and strength of character that is antithetical to letting up, giving in, or "throwing in the towel." *Steadfastness* implies "unwavering," "unvarying," "loyal," and "single-minded purpose" leading to the achievement of a goal. If I am to "press forward with a steadfastness in Christ," I must bear down and keep pushing unwaveringly toward my single goal—to be more like the Savior. Nephi's words *in Christ* remind me that I am not alone in my quest for that goal, and when I fall down and fall short and feel that I can never make it, the Lord is there to lift and guide and strengthen me. "Each time you fall He will pick you up again," wrote C. S. Lewis. "And He knows perfectly well that your own efforts are never going to bring you anywhere near [His] perfection."

> On the other hand, you must realise from the outset that the goal toward which He is beginning to guide you is absolute perfection; and no power in the whole universe, except you yourself, can prevent Him from taking you to that goal. . . .
>
> The command *Be ye perfect* [and we as Latter-day Saints might add—"What manner of men ought ye to be? Verily I say unto you, even as I am"] is not idealistic gas. Nor is it a command to do the impossible. He is going to make us into creatures that can obey that command. He said (in the Bible) that we were "gods" and He is going to make good His words. If we let Him—for we can prevent Him, if we choose—He will make the feeblest and filthiest of us into a god or goddess, dazzling, radiant, immortal creature, pulsating all through with such energy and joy and wisdom and love as we cannot now imagine, a bright stainless mirror which reflects back to God perfectly . . . His own boundless power and delight and goodness. The process will be long and in parts very painful; but that is what we are in for. Nothing less. He meant what He said. (*Mere Christianity* [New York: Macmillan, 1960], pp. 172, 174–75.)

Several years ago I saw a remarkable example of physical courage and strength that taught me a deeper spiritual meaning of what it means to press forward in steadfastness and to endure to the end. During the 1984 summer Olympics held in Los Angeles, we saw on our television screens a remarkable sight. It was both disturbing and inspiring at the same time. A contestant in the women's marathon staggered into the coliseum suffering from the strain, severe heat exhaustion, and the fatigue of the twenty-six-mile-race. She was many minutes behind the medalists, but she was intent on finishing. It was painful to watch her struggling to stay on her feet. She staggered like a drunkard. She could not run but merely tried to keep moving—to keep putting one foot in front of the other. It was obvious to the world-wide television audience that she was not only desperately trying to finish the race but also struggling to remain conscious. It seemed to take forever for her to complete the last few yards of the race. Olympic officials tried to assist her and to get her to stop, for fear that she might seriously injure herself if she continued under such conditions. She waved them off, however, and kept on moving. She exemplified in a most remarkable way what I think Nephi meant by the phrase *press forward*. However difficult it was to watch her struggle and stagger, it was inspiring to witness her courage and determination. She just would not quit. Her performance was more awe-inspiring than that of the gold medalist. Fans in the coliseum rose to their feet in a thundering ovation to acknowledge her monumental accomplishment. When it would have been easy and perhaps logical to quit, she kept going, one staggering step at a time, until she collapsed across the finish line.

Striving to become more like Christ can also be compared to running a marathon: It is a long, arduous process made up of pressing forward one step after another. The marathon runner receives assistance to help him or her in the quest to finish. There are refreshment stops where the runner is handed drinks to prevent dehydration and cramping up. There are coaches to instruct and motivate. Loved ones and fans cheer and exhort the runner on toward the finish line. Despite all these aids, the ultimate goal of finishing the race can be obtained solely by the runner. The only thing that will prevent him or her from reaching the finish line is to give up and stop running.

We too have others to assist us and encourage us along the way in our quest to become more Christlike. When we get discouraged and spiritually fatigued—when it seems we can't take another step—the Lord is mindful of us and he does not forsake us. In his infinite love and mercy, he has provided a means to help us to press forward and to keep our eyes focused on the finish line. Always remembering him is the means that keeps us moving toward our goal. "To become as He is, we must have Him constantly in our thoughts," President Ezra Taft Benson taught. "Every time we partake of the sacrament we covenant to always remember Him" (Moroni 4:3; 5:2; D&C 20:77, 79). If thoughts make us what we are and we are to be like Christ, then we must think Christlike thoughts." (*Come Unto Christ* [Salt Lake City: Deseret Book Co., 1983], p. 41.)

Each week as we partake of the sacrament of the Lord's Supper, we covenant to keep his commandments and to always remember him. Remembering involves not just recounting his life and ministry in our minds but also taking inventory of our lives. We ask ourselves, How am I doing in my quest to be more Christlike? Have I fallen short this week? What can I do better this coming week? Not only do we renew our covenant to keep the commandments, but also, as we partake of the symbols of Christ's flesh and blood, we can commune with God and petition him for strength and direction in our lives. "Try to remember," the familiar song refrains, "and if you remember, then follow." Always remembering Christ is a catalyst for following him. Remembering what he did for me and how he lived his life prods me forward in love to walk more closely in his footsteps. Remembering him is covenanting—covenanting that I will keep trying to be more Christlike no matter how wide the gap may seem between me and the Ideal; covenanting to strive to be even a little better tomorrow than I was today; covenanting to be more kind, compassionate, loving, and forgiving. As I remember him I can earnestly pray for and diligently seek more holiness in my life.

More holiness give me,
More strivings within,
More patience in suff'ring,
More sorrow for sin,
More faith in my Savior,
More sense of his care,
More joy in his service,
More purpose in prayer.

More gratitude give me,
More trust in the Lord,
More pride in his glory,
More hope in his word,
More tears for his sorrows,
More pain at his grief,
More meekness in trial,
More praise for relief.

More purity give me,
More strength to o'ercome,
More freedom from earthstains,
More longing for home.
More fit for the kingdom,
More used would I be,
More blessed and holy—
More, Savior, like thee.
(Philip Paul Bliss, "More Holiness Give Me,"
in *Hymns,* no. 131.)

This sacred and spiritual weekly ordinance reminds us that we have taken up the cross and committed ourselves to a determined discipleship, and therefore we cannot give up or look back. Not only does this ordinance remind us and prods us forward, it protects us as well. "No man goes away from this Church and becomes an apostate in a week or in a month," Elder Melvin J. Ballard said. "It is a slow process. The one thing that would make for the safety of every man and woman would be to appear at the sacrament table every Sabbath day. We would not get very far away in one week—not so far away that, by the process of self-investigation, we could not rectify the wrongs we may have done. If we should refrain from partaking of the sacrament, condemned by ourselves as unworthy to receive these emblems, we could not endure that long, and we would soon, I am sure, have the spirit of repentance. The road to the sacrament table is the path of safety for Latter-day Saints." (*Melvin J. Ballard . . . Crusader for Righteousness* [Salt Lake City: Bookcraft, 1966], p. 134.)

While serving as a bishop, I gained a greater appreciation for the power of the sacrament to keep our minds and hearts centered upon the Savior and to keep us ever pressing forward in our quest to become more like him. Whenever it became necessary because of transgression to put a ward member on probation and to preclude him or her from partaking of the sacrament, I would never attach a time period to that restriction. For example, I never would say, "Don't partake of the sacrament for two weeks or a month." Instead I would counsel, "I don't want you to partake of the sacrament until further notice." For some people that "further notice" was longer in coming than for others, but in every case I saw how the absence of the sacrament not only enriched the repentance process but also instilled in them a greater desire to live more like the Savior so they could once again partake of the symbols of his flesh and blood. When a ward member so disciplined would come back and ask, "Bishop, how much longer? I really want to partake of the sacrament," I knew that they had felt the void in their lives that comes from not partaking of that holy ordinance and that they now were truly "hungering and thirsting after righteousness." They desired to feel of the Lord's cleansing power, and in *remembering* him they were now ready to commit to *following* him.

Over and over again I saw how the sacrament is a very real agent of change. It not only reminds us of him, but beckons us to come unto him by striving to live like him and in turn partake of the "Bread of Life" and the "Living Waters." When properly understood, we see in the sacrament one of God's greatest means to draw us unto his Only Begotten Son. Through humble introspection, we see our weaknesses. Through repentance and recommitment, we experience the transformation that comes through the Atonement. Through remembering Christ and his divine attributes, we learn what we must do to pattern our lives after him. Through covenanting to always remember him and to keep his commandments, we keep moving forward to that end. The sacred ordinance of the sacrament is a means whereby we "press forward with a steadfastness in Christ" toward our goal of more Christlike living, loving, and leading.

I received a call late one Saturday evening from a ward member. "Bishop, my wife really needs to talk to you," the husband said. We made arrangements to meet at the bishop's office first thing in the morning. The next day the husband and wife arrived at the church hand in hand, but with eyes swollen and red from a night of crying. It seemed like an eternity before she was able to speak. When the words finally came, they flowed like a raging river that had just burst a dam. She had carried with her the heavy burden of sin for many years. She had been promiscuous before she met her husband. He was a worthy young man and was wonderful to her. After their engagement, they prepared themselves spiritually for a temple marriage. Yet she was carrying some heavy spiritual baggage. Neither her bishop nor her stake president had interviewed her thoroughly, assuming that she was worthy in every way—and she certainly appeared and acted as if she was. Immature and frightened at the time, she reasoned, *If they don't ask, I don't have to tell.* So she went to the temple unworthily. Hiding her past from her husband as well as her priesthood leaders, she continued to live a lie. In the years since her immoral past, she had tried so hard to be as Christlike as she could. She was one of the most pure in heart I had met. If I hadn't heard her confession with my own ears, I could never have imagined her so deeply in sin.

"I know that I will probably have to be excommunicated," she sobbed. "But I cannot carry this burden and live this lie any longer." Her heart was broken and her spirit truly contrite. She sobbed about the pain she had caused her husband when she told him of her shady past—all completely hidden from him through the years. Yet he loved her so much, and so desired her to be made spiritually whole, that it was he who had called me and lovingly taken her by the hand to the bishop's office.

"I don't know if excommunication will be necessary," I tried to explain to her. "Before I can make any decision about what to do, I would like you to kneel with me and let's seek the guidance of our Heavenly Father." I poured out my heart in her behalf and pleaded with the Lord to direct me in how I could best help her find forgiveness. I asked that if it was necessary that I hold a bishop's disciplinary council for her, that he would let me know. During the course of that prayer a remarkable thing ocurred—at least, for me it was rare and remarkable. The Spirit clearly taught me and I knew beyond a doubt what to do. There were no words or angelic beings, just a strong impression to my soul. I knew the will of God and knew what he would have me do and say.

It was revealed to me that this woman had carried a tremendous burden of guilt through the years, yet had diligently tried to reform her life. The years since her marriage had been devoted to service in the Church and seeking to emulate the Savior in every way possible. The whispering of the still, small voice testified to me that her confession was now the end of her repentance process, not the beginning. There was no need for a disciplinary council—that prompting defied every ounce of logic and preconceived ideas that I had had before we knelt together in prayer. As I told her what I felt, the tears once again flowed freely, this time from relief and gratitude but also from the confirming witness of the Spirit. I then proceeded to give her some counsel that had clearly been given to me by the power of the Holy Ghost.

"Ordinarily I would ask you not to partake of the sacrament under these circumstances," I explained, "but the Spirit has commanded me to counsel you to partake of the sacrament today and to think deeply of what the Savior has done for you. I promise you that you will feel this burden lifted, and spiritual healing will come into your soul."

During sacrament meeting, as we sang the sacrament hymn, I couldn't take my eyes off of her. It was almost as if I could see into her spirit and witness the transformation firsthand. I could see there was more meaning in the words of the hymn to her than to the rest of the congregation. After the sacramental prayers were offered, there was the usual reverent silence as ward members pondered on the life of the Savior and his atoning sacrifice. I felt that she possessed a depth of "remembering him" that, at least for that moment, was unsurpassed in the chapel. My heart was full to overflowing as I watched her partake of the bread and then bury her head in the shoulder of her husband. I could see her shoulders and body shudder as she wept. She wept almost uncontrollably, but her tears were tears of joy as she smiled into the eyes of her loving and forgiving eternal companion. It was clear that the burden was lifted. I was witness to a miracle—the miracle of forgiveness, the miracle of spiritual healing. Never before had the sacrament meant so much to me. After the meeting, she approached me and I knew she wanted to express appreciation, but the words couldn't make their way past the lumps in our throats. She threw her arms around me and we just cried together. We knew. We knew.

In the years since that event, I have thought about it many times and have witnessed similar scenes of spiritual healing and rededication resulting from sacramental covenants. I am grateful beyond expression for this sacred ordinance that gives me a regular opportunity to remember Christ and rededicate myself to becoming more like him. In the quiet moments during the sacrament, I have experienced the power of revelation teaching me about him, about me, and what I need to do to more faithfully walk in his footsteps. It is not just covenantal renewal, it is truly a time to remember him; "and if you remember, then follow." This covenantal remembering—intellectual remembrance coupled with spiritual rededication and repentance—leads us to continually think on Christ and to strive to be like him. "And now, O man," King Benjamin admonished, "remember, and perish not" (Mosiah 4:30).

We must know Christ better than we know him;
we must remember him more often than we remember him;
we must serve him more valiantly than we serve him.
Then we will drink water springing up unto eternal life
and will eat the bread of life.
What manner of men and women ought we to be?
Even as he is.
—President Howard W. Hunter

As we press forward with steadfastness in Christ, there will be bumps and bruises along the way. There will be discouragement and disappointment because we just don't measure up as much as we would like or because our progress toward Christlike living isn't more rapid. But if we will always remember Christ, we will not—we cannot—give up, for he not only is the Perfect Exemplar but is also "the way, the truth, and the Life" (John 14:6). May we always remember him by seeking always to follow him and by striving to become like him. "There is no greater, more thrilling, and more soul-enobling challenge," declared President Ezra Taft Benson, "than to try to learn of Christ and walk in His steps."

> He walked this earth as our Exemplar. He is our Advocate with the Father. He worked out the great atoning sacrifice so we could have a fulness of joy and be exalted in accordance with His grace and our repentance and righteousness. He did all things perfectly and commands that we be perfect even as He and His Father are perfect. (See 3 Nephi 12:48.)

"What would Jesus do?" or "What would He have me do?" are the paramount personal questions of this life. Walking in His way is the greatest achievement of life.

That man or woman is most truly successful whose life most closely parallels that of the Master.

Let us look to Him in every thought.

Think on Christ! (In *Come Unto Christ,* pp. 46–47.)

INDEX

— K —

— L —

— M —